angry
BIRDS killer
& BEES

angry
BIRDS *killer*
& BEES

talking to your kids
about sex

Todd Bowman

BEACON HILL PRESS
OF KANSAS CITY

CONTENTS

Section One

SEX
MYTHS AND MESSAGES

one

HIGH VOLTAGE!

aution! Reading this book may change your life.

If you picked up this book, it's likely you have a child or two who will be ready to have "the talk" in the near future, and you're arming yourself with the courage and details necessary to successfully navigate the unknown waters of talking with your kids about sex.

First, thank you for your willingness to take on the parental responsibility of educating your children about their bodies and the purposes for which they are intended; and second—hang on. Stewarding our children's sexuality is a skill set that has been lost, and a multitude of voices are willing to serve that role for parents if parents remain silent. The educational system attempts to assist parents in this process but operates from a different worldview—or lens—than that of most Christians. Simply knowing enough to identify what the parts do, where they go, and what happens when the parts intersect is not the ideal version of "the talk." Parents must talk to their children about the emotional and spiritual dimensions of sexuality rather than just the physical aspects.

Unfortunately, alarming numbers of parents are abdicating this responsibility to the health-class teachers of middle school and high school students across the country.

Another culprit in educating children about sex is the media. Not just the tabloids, Hollywood, and *Playboy,* but *all* types of media. YouTube, Facebook, iTunes, Spotify, Vine, and other products offer an endless supply of seemingly innocent material, the vast majority of which is laden with tremendous sexual innuendo and the blatant objectification of other people as things.

Late Stanford psychologist Al Cooper in discussing the rise of Internet pornography coined the phrase "triple-A engine" to describe why this trend grows at such a rapid pace. The three As in the triple-A engine are *accessibility, affordability,* and *anonymity.*[1] Cooper proposed that these three variables accounted for the enormous growth in pornography use with the birth of the Internet in the early 1990s.

These three drivers of the growth in pornography use in Western civilization extend well beyond the computer. Music with lyrics about promiscuity and sexuality are abundant and can be accessed for free without anyone knowing. A great example of this is Rhianna's song titled "S&M," which depicts sexual connection as a violent exchange of pain and pleasure, devoid of much connective emotional content. While inaccessible on YouTube, a brief search for this song on Google provides access to a world of sexuality that is certain to taint an adolescent or teenager's understanding of what healthy sexuality entails. And the content that is accessible on YouTube provides a much darker look into the world of commercial sexuality that sweeps away many children and adolescents.

Other cultural influencers, including Mark Laaser of Faithful and True in Eden Prairie, Minnesota, a leading Christian sexual addiction specialist, have added a fourth "A" to Cooper's initial theory: *accidental.* Easy as it may be to envision a six-year-old stumbling across an inappropriate Web site while conducting a search for a favorite cartoon character, what is accidental to a child is not accidental to the industry that is looking to get its product in front of as many consumers as possible—at younger and younger ages. Porn users of yesteryear bought it from adult bookstores or convenience stores. Now, porn seeks out potential users by trolling the Internet, gaming sites, and e-mail. For example, <www.coke.com> was a pornography Web site until Coca-Cola purchased back the domain name for a staggering amount of money. Web sites such as <pokemon.com>, <whitehouse.com>, and others have been used to "accidentally" expose young children to depictions of human sexuality that are incongruent with the child's development, opening a Pandora's Box in the minds of young boys and girls.[2]

The video game industry is another arena in which the pornography industry targets young consumers. Forget Vegas; in the life of a fourteen-year-old boy, what happens online stays online. Unfortunately this is not true. We carry many of those shocking yet simultaneously pleasing images with us across our lifetimes, seeking to explore the curiosities and possibilities we are exposed to. The average age of exposure to pornographic content is eleven years of age—and getting younger.[3]

Another area in which media sends subtle yet powerful messages about sexuality is through children's movies. Messages regarding sexuality are present in a variety of forms. One variety of influence is the music that is selected for inclusion in films.

As in most families, my children have watched a variety of G or PG animated movies without much prescreening. (You are shocked to hear this, I know.) As an aside, the Internet Movie Database (<imdb.com>) provides a great resource for reviewing movies for language, violence and gore, sexual content/nudity, drug-and-alcohol-related content, and frightening or graphic images before you watch them.

I was made aware of the impact of the music that is included in children's movies one Sunday night after our small-group meeting. My older son, who was five at the time, was having a great time playing with the daughter of our friends from our small group. They had run laps around the house during the group meeting, had come down for snacks and drinks, and were playing again when it came time for her family to leave. As we were saying our goodbyes for the evening, I heard my son invite his friend upstairs to the playroom. "I want to show you something," he said with enthusiasm. The two of them slipped toward the steps, not realizing I had overheard their conversation and had crept silently up the steps behind them. As I observed them, my fears were assuaged by the fact that my son was simply showing her his favorite new toy with his famous "isn't-it-awesome" voice.

I announced my presence with a simple question—"What are you all doing up here?" Startled, my son, who was still red in the face from all the running and wearing too many layers of clothes, made a somewhat silly face at his friend and sang the lyrics "I'm sexy and I know it" while stripping off his outer layer of clothing, a heavy sweater. For the sake of full disclosure, I have to admit that my initial response was to laugh. It was one of those incredibly cute moments involving your kids that you carry with you forever.

The shock and laughter quickly turned to concern: *When did Magic Mike move in with me, and what happened to my innocent five-year-old?* I thought. Upon further investigation, it turns out that the music he was singing came from a movie my wife and I had introduced him to, *Madagascar 3*. I would be remiss if I tried to convince you that this failure as a parent was my only failure; however, we were able to turn the experience into a conversation about modesty and his body, appropriate relationships with the opposite sex, and what *sexy* even means.

The lesson that we took away from this experience is that while we cannot necessarily control the content that enters our children's lives (although we do filter much of it), we are responsible for helping them understand what the content is suggesting and how this content stands against the truths of Scripture, even when it's silly or seemingly innocent. With movies such as Disney's *Brave,* in which adults' and children's bare buttocks are visually depicted, we must recognize that the messages being sent to our children about the innocence of nudity only ups the ante. Stewarding their sexuality will become more difficult, because the messages they receive from the culture around them will become more intense.

Back to my previous word of caution: while this book is certainly designed to help equip you to engage in a more intentional and thorough version of "the talk"—think of it of more as "the conversation"—with your children at a variety of ages and stages, it will also force you to complete two other difficult tasks: (1) exploring your own sexual past and development and (2) discussing sexuality in the context of your spousal relationship (if applicable). Before initiating "the conversation," it is important to invest yourself into the task of exploring any potential areas of interference that might come up that have little to do with your kids and much more to do with your own story.

Our American culture has developed an uncanny ability to avoid the process of exploring our own experiences. Denial of the past, projecting our own shortcomings or faults onto others, and simply displacing our anger, fear, shame, and sadness have become commonplace. I'll sum it up in one terrifying yet familiar catchphrase—"It wasn't me"—which also happens to be the phrase for a graphically disturbing song from years past. While there may be some truth to the fact that we inherit a variety of concerns and potential problems from choices made by others that in no way involved us—such as abuse, neglect, molestation, and others—the fact remains that it is our responsibility to seek healing and take ownership for *our responses to those choices*, whether those previous injuries and abuses were initiated by a spouse or someone else. When it comes to exploring our previous sexual experiences, these defense mechanisms tend to manifest themselves with an intensity seen in few other circumstances, sometimes more so within the church than outside it. And our spouse is the one bearing the brunt of the impact.

Think back to your early sexual experiences for a moment. Let yourself re-experience the gentle touch of holding hands. Did you know that the largest organ is skin and is tied closely to sexuality? Your heart pounded in your chest the first time your fingers locked, and your mind raced with excitement. Then came the first kiss. Your heart pounded even faster this time, and perhaps you became intoxicated with emotion at the experience of your lips meeting another's for the first time. These experiences create a powerful neurological experience that is nearly impossible to duplicate.

The purpose of this experience is to facilitate pair bonding, or attachment, which is a state of physical, emotional, and spiritual closeness in the relationship. At sixteen we are likely to believe these bonds will never rupture and that the "love" we are experiencing will transcend any challenge that life can throw at us. We fail to realize in these mostly innocent adolescent moments that our hormones are driving the bus, and the feelings we experience are predominantly induced by a neurohormone known as phenylethylamine or PEA, which is a hallucinogen.[4] Love struck, we believe that this high will last forever. Then life throws us the curveball of breakup, divorce, or severed relationship, and the delusion is shattered by the coldness of reality.

Unfortunately, all of us have been forced to experience the pain of rupture at some point. Reflect now, if you will, on the experience of losing the relationship in which "love" blossomed. Experience again the sadness, perhaps even despair, you experienced at the thought of no longer being connected to this significant other with whom you first held hands or shared that special kiss. The intensity and excitement of those early experiences gave way to the hurt of brokenness and fear of never being loved again. This experience is difficult enough to navigate on its own; add a high-pleasure, high-shame-based experience like sexual exploration, and the stakes—and consequences—get even higher. An association has been made, a bond has been forged, and bonds are difficult to undo once they have been experienced, which is why you can recall many of these powerful experiences almost as if they were yesterday.

If there is a sense of shame surrounding these sexual encounters from an earlier developmental period in your life, you are not alone. Many whom I have counseled in my years as a therapist have early shame-based sexual experiences that they have been unable to escape. Shame has a subtle influence in our cognitive and emotional functioning. Specifically, we see shame as the root of avoidance in relationship with others. Consider the following passage from Genesis 3:6-10—

When the woman saw that the fruit of the tree was good for food and pleasing to the eye, and also desirable for gaining wisdom, she took some and ate it. She also gave some to her husband, who was with her, and he ate it. Then the eyes of both of them were opened, and they realized they were naked; so they sewed fig leaves together and made coverings for themselves.

Then the man and his wife heard the sound of the LORD God as he was walking in the garden in the cool of the day, and they hid from the LORD God among the trees of the garden. But the LORD God called to the man, "Where are you?"

He answered, "I heard you in the garden, and I was afraid because I was naked; so I hid."

In the biblical narrative and in everyday life, shame serves the same essential function: covering and hiding. They made coverings for themselves to hide their nakedness, and they hid in the garden when God walked among them.

When I was younger, probably ten or eleven, my brother had a birthday coming up, which meant one thing: birthday mail— and not just birthday mail but birthday mail with birthday *money!* On this particular day I raced home to the mailbox, and to my excitement, in the mail was a birthday card for my brother from our great-grandmother. Birthday money! However, rather than racing inside and handing the card to my brother, I raced up to my room with the stolen loot, eager to claim my prize.

Much to my disappointment, when I opened the card, there was a check for ten dollars inside. A ten-year-old cannot do much with a check; so to cover my tracks I did what most lazy children that age do—I tore it up and threw it in my mess of a closet, where I believed it was gone for eternity. No more shame! In that closet, my mind convinced me that it was as far as the east is from the west. Buried, never again to rear its ugly head and remind me of my cowardice and greed.

At least it was buried until a few months later, when I had failed to clean my room after repeated requests. My parents, much to their dismay, I'm certain, physically assisted me in completing this seemingly enormous task. We cleaned under the bed, in my dresser, and eventually in the closet, where my transgression had lain silently for months to the point that I had forgotten its existence.

My father found the first piece and inquired, "What is this?" The sickening grip of shame began to encroach on my digestive system. "I don't know" was all I could muster, and my mind raced back to that fateful afternoon. Within minutes the full knowledge of my deed had been discovered, and shame drove me to the darkest corner I could escape to: under my bed—which was now accessible to me, ironically enough.

I covered myself, and I hid. My shame was as smothering as the space I had shrunken into. Tearfully, I recounted what I had done, and my parents set out to make amends with my brother, who had no awareness that anything had transpired. I lay there in the darkness, weeping.

It is quite easy as parents to unknowingly live a life of shame, simply discounting our past experiences and praying our children never discover the brokenness we once embodied or perhaps that which we currently experience. How quickly we disengage from conversations pertaining to sexuality because of the painful or shameful memories from our own pasts! In the general public most people are afraid to discuss suicide, because they believe that actively discussing suicide makes individuals with suicidal thoughts more likely to attempt the act.

We know that the reverse is true. Having open discussion about suicide actually prevents suicide attempts among the general population. As neuroscientist Dan Siegel states in his book *The Whole-Brain Child*, we must "name it to tame it."[5] When things exist in secrecy, they have enormous power in our lives. In the church and in good Christian homes I fear we have bought into a similar lie: if we discuss sexuality, our children or our youth group members will go and experiment sexually. If we teach them about it, they will go try it.

This myth, which paralyzes parents and pastors alike, perpetuates the shame children feel about sexuality, because it remains something secret, something dirty, or something taboo. Growing healthy children must begin with a vulnerability and willingness to share our brokenness with them, ideally in appropriate ways and at appropriate times in their development, which we will eventually explore together. We must talk with them about the gift that God has given us in sex so that they understand the sacramental nature of sexuality and how to steward it well. If you are living a shame-saturated life due to unfortunate sexual experiences, no matter how valiant your attempts to protect your children from the consequences you continue to experience, they will ultimately bear the weight of it. Through counseling, spiritual direction with a pastor, and support groups in the church or the community, you must find healing so that you can steward your children's sexuality from a place of completeness. One of the truisms from the counseling field is "Hurting people hurt people." A parent who struggles with sexual brokenness is ultimately likely to raise a child with a similar sexual brokenness.

If you have made it to this point in the book, I applaud you for facing some uncomfortable content. If you need to take a break and process through some of the memories and/or emotions that have emerged during your reading, I would encourage you to do that. Call a friend and process what you're thinking and feeling. Open a journal and write expressively. Take a long walk or jog and allow your mind to wander and sift through everything. Whatever you do, please do not bury anything you have experienced. The path to wholeness for yourself and for the well-being of your children starts with your confronting memories that have perhaps been long buried. Shame would have you cover yourself with half-truths and hide your story behind veiled secrets, but there is no freedom in shame—only loneliness and despair. Know that you are not alone in responding to this content in that way; bring those things that you have covered or hidden for so long into the light of disclosure, and find healing by reaching out to trusted companions and loved ones.

Now that you have had a chance to reflect on your past, take a deep breath, and prepare yourself for digging into the next layer of content. Discussing sexuality in the marriage relationship also unearths previous hurts and disappointments that frequently inhibit teaching children about sexuality. Wounds from issues such as unmet sexual expectations as far as excitement or frequency of intercourse and discovered betrayals such as pornography or infidelity create a pain that causes us to shrink away from actively engaging our children in discussion about human sexuality.

In fact, the nature of the marriage relationship creates a context in which many of the painful, scary, shameful, and otherwise unpleasant experiences you reflected on in the previous section are brought to the present moment and re-experienced. But rather than having a corrective influence in your life, the relationship that was designed to be a source of safety, trust, and intimacy eventually becomes another source of injury. Many of the stories I hear in my clinical practice provide insight into this relational reality. Perhaps one of these is similar to your story.

> My father was a perfectionist, and I never felt I could do anything to make him happy. Now I feel the same way with John, my husband. According to him, I am "never interested enough in sex" or "never willing to try new things." All I feel when I think about our sex life is that I do not measure up, that I am a failure, and that it will never change. He is just like my father.

Or maybe this story is similar to yours:

"Hovering" doesn't even begin to describe my mother's presence in my life. While I appreciated the help at an early age, at some point I just learned to disengage and stop caring. Mom was going to do it for me even if I *wanted* to do it myself. There was never space for me to grow up, which I am a little angry about, I guess. Now I feel the same way about my sex life. Even though I want to connect sexually with my wife, I don't want to face the rejection. She runs the marriage, and when she is ready for sex, she will let me know. I guess I am a little angry about that as well.

Or—

I don't feel as if I ever learned to be a sexual person until I was a teenager. I never saw my parents showing one another affection. They never sat on the couch together, never hugged, never held hands, never kissed in front of us kids. I learned about sex from other places, such as my friends and pornography. Whatever I was curious about, there was an answer just a click away. When I got married, my expectations were based on the videos I had seen and stories I had heard, not the reality of the woman in front of me and her emotional and spiritual needs. I really hurt her with the things I introduced into our sexual relationship. I wish I could take them back.

Or—

For me sex was a gateway to affection. It helped me become popular, keep boyfriends, and even get promoted. Men cared about me more when I was giving them sex. . . . When I got married, sex became a way to get what I wanted. I traded sex to feel cared for. I still have a hard time believing that love can be "unconditional."

Sex has become a commodity in American culture. It has become detached from its created purposes, perverted, and dangles before us as some prize to be won or escape to be found. And to make things more difficult, redeeming sexuality within the church is an uphill battle.

Stewarding our children's sexuality well is perhaps one of the most uncomfortable, confusing, embarrassing, rewarding responsibilities we will ever have. For us to be able to fulfill this role well, we must explore our sexual history for lingering assumptions or injuries as they shape if and how we teach and talk about sex.

Many of you will be the first in generations—maybe ever—to broach the topic with your children. Good! To do this you must establish a place of safety and trust in the marriage relationship that corrects some of the filth—false assumptions, negative experiences, and unrealistic expectations—that culture has worked into you. Through spouses engaging one another in open conversation about sex in their own marriage, the Holy Spirit begins the process of working out that which the world has worked into you; you can finally find the healing and freedom you've been looking for. When you initiate this important conversation with your children, you become co-participants with the Holy Spirit in that process for them.

The following questions are for reflection and discussion before you initiate "the conversation" with your children. You may wish to discuss these with your spouse, and professional counseling may be appropriate depending on your responses.

1. What sexual experiences have you never disclosed to anyone? How do these experiences shape your sexual relationship in your marriage? Who is someone trustworthy you could share your story with?

2. How has sex been negotiated in your marriage to this point? Is it mutually agreed upon?

3. How comfortable do you feel conversing with your spouse about your sex life?

   a. Not at all comfortable

b. Somewhat comfortable

c. Mostly comfortable

d. Very comfortable

4. What sexual practices in the relationship make you uncomfortable? Where did these practices originate—inside the relationship or before the relationship began, such as in teenage or college years, with a different partner? Have you voiced your feelings?

5. What safeguards do you have in place to keep sexual temptation from impacting your marriage relationship? Internet filtering software? Men's and women's accountability groups? Something else?

two
SEX
TALKS

M om, Dad, what's sex?" This is one question all of us dread
our children asking as we watch them grow and change.
We're left feeling as if we're tumbling down a rabbit hole
and into a foreign land fraught with potentially embarrassing
self-disclosures and graphic words we don't want our children
ever to hear, let alone speak, a land where we'll have to teach our
children about the parts of their bodies and parts of our marriages we rarely discuss. Layer in the awkwardness you feel about
your son's or daughter's changing body and his or her curiosity
about sexual activity, and the desire to avoid this conversation
at all costs shoots through the roof. The simple fact is this: sex
isn't talked about in most American families. Kids are doing it,
without a doubt, but it isn't discussed.

While we don't really talk about sex in our culture, we see sex everywhere. Sexualized images exist in movies, on television, on the Internet, in video games, at the mall, in magazines, in our e-mail, on our cell phones. Sex has been used to sell hamburgers, cars, Web sites, underwear, toothpaste—you name it. Basically, sex has been used in some way, shape, or form to sell just about everything. If we open our eyes, we're hard-pressed to get through a single day without being exposed to sexual material of some sort.

But with all this sexual content available to us at any given moment, it's a topic we rarely actually discuss with our spouses and our friends. Difficulty talking about sex in these contexts makes it extremely difficult to find the comfort and courage necessary to talk with our kids about it. By leaving them in the dark, we leave them to learn everything they know about sex from the movies they watch, from the conversations they have at school, and from what they see depicted in pornography.

If you're like most people, the last thing you want to think about is the fact that your child may have been exposed to sexual material, your child has actively sought out a sexual experience of some sort, or at some point in their lives your children will encounter some message about sex. For a culture that is very much addicted to sex, we rarely actually *talk* about sex.

Sex in American culture has been boiled down to a cocktail of body parts and bodily functions, wacky experimentation, and personal pleasure. If Hollywood and the media are the only sources teaching our children about sex, they are at risk of living lives terribly devoid of the intimacy that sex is designed to enhance, including our understanding of God and his relationship with us. In a nutshell, we have been so desensitized to the sexual content available in our culture and so disconnected from the assault on our children that we do little to stop it.

To top it all, add in a healthy dose of shame that exists within the church that pushes our sexual attitudes and behaviors further underground, and you have a recipe for raising a child who has a lifelong struggle with believing the myths and distortions of human sexuality in American culture. Rather than shaming and blaming, we need to connect and redirect our kids and their understanding of healthy sexuality.[1]

As we know, sex embodies a variety of physical acts that involve the identification and exploration of that which brings us pleasure. However, the mainstream depictions of sexual activity our children are regularly exposed to rarely embody anything more than sex. Television and movies depict sex as multiple sexual partners and frequent random hookups. There is actually now an app for that. If you have not looked into the MTV show *Skins* to see how sex is depicted for teenagers today, I urge you to take a look. You will be shocked and appalled by what you find. That is just the tip of the iceberg.

In these forms of media, the physical aspects of human sexuality are depicted with gross inaccuracy. The glaring and primary absence in these scenes is the corresponding emotional and spiritual dynamics that work together to complete the definition of what it truly means to be sexual.

Take a second to think of the last sexual scene you were exposed to in a movie. Do you have one in mind? My guess is that the emphasis had very little to do with emotional or spiritual connection—and a lot more to do with physical pleasure. Now think of the last scene you are aware of that your child was exposed to. Does your child have the foundation to understand and make sense of the messages that were being sent? Do you have the foundation to make sense of what is healthy and what is unhealthy about what he or she saw?

When children believe that the physical aspects of sex are divorced from the emotional and spiritual, they are vulnerable to being taken captive by the pleasurable thoughts, feelings, and physical sensations offered by sexual experiences. They can escape for a moment into the ecstasy—only to come crashing back to reality after a fleeting moment of pleasure. With the crash comes a heavy guilt, a dark shame, and an intense anxiety as their despair and disconnection from healthy relationships grows. Much like a piece of candy that tastes sweet for a moment but is ultimately unable to satisfy our hunger, sex, when experienced as simply a physical experience, fails to fulfill our desires. When devoid of its inherent spiritual and emotional essence, sex is as empty as the vacancy in the soul it is used to fill. If we are to raise our children to make healthy sexual choices, it is imperative that they are given information to compete with the messages communicated to them by American culture.

What Constitutes Sex These Days?

Given the variety in the depictions of sex, one question that comes up quite frequently for children and adolescents is "What is sex?" It is typically phrased something like this: "What really counts as sex?" Recent history in our culture makes the claim that intercourse and other sexual acts are different constructs. The confusion experienced by adolescents about what constitutes sex is driven by the disconnection we see between the words and actions of celebrities and politicians: Tiger Woods and his mistresses, the University of Miami football team and its involvement with a prostitution ring, the Minnesota Vikings sex boat scandal, politicians in bathrooms and on the Internet, teachers and their students, ministers—and the list goes on. Despite claims that intercourse and other sexual activities are fundamentally different, our brains tell us they are one and the same.

Sexual activity is sexual activity, and the younger kids are when they become involved in sexual activity, the more likely they are to abuse drugs and alcohol, break the law, and take part in other problematic behavior.[2]

Oral sex, pornography, and masturbation are the three primary experiences that teens are referring to when they ask this question. While many believe that their relationship with their boyfriend or girlfriend contains the depth of emotional and spiritual connection necessary to delve into sexual exploration, the truth is they do not. When sex is defined as intercourse only, it opens a world of possibilities for exploring sexuality without actually "having sex."

One thing that oral sex, pornography, and masturbation have in common is that they are more focused on individual pleasure than enhancing the attachment bond that comes through the marriage partnership. Helping children understand that emotionally and spiritually healthy relationships do not depend on the cheap imitation of acceptance or desirability offered by these sexual acts is a critical step. As you can see, when we use the terms *sex* and *intercourse* synonymously, the door opens for our children to engage in a variety of sexual acts without the healthy sense of guilt or shame. The social pressure on them to participate in these activities is so great that over half cave in and join the crowd by the age of seventeen,[3] as we will see in chapter five.

Engaging "the conversation" about sex provides a lifeline for our children to have a safe place to come and ask questions, learn what is healthy, and alleviate the pressure they feel to participate in these behaviors to fit in.

Feelings—Nothing More than Feelings

Because of the guilt and shame many kids feel when they have engaged in sexual behavior, they instinctively move toward other behaviors that distract them from what their God-given design tells them—that this is not right. It is a vicious cycle. The behaviors vary from person to person, but all facilitate the same numbness to escape the shame and guilt: drinking and drug use, angry music, excessive spending, cutting, disordered eating, excessive video gaming, gambling. Our culture teaches us to trade one source of shame for another, putting ourselves on the path toward addictions of all sorts. If your child manifests these behaviors, has frequent mood swings for no apparent reason, or isolates for hours on end, facilitate a conversation about sex sooner rather than later. Professional help may be warranted.

On the flip side, we have a healthier definition of sex. Sex, in the appropriate relational context of marriage, is designed to serve as the culmination of time spent in spiritual, emotional, and physical closeness in the work of living life together. It is the opportunity to experience and share the deepest levels of vulnerability with each another and to embrace a closeness with each other that cannot be had any other way. With that closeness comes a commitment to mutual well-being and a mature love that seeks to enhance the other. Physically, there is the joining together to become one flesh as the male and female bodies give and receive in their respective designs. An acceptance is found, one that transcends our physical bodies and touches the very emotional and spiritual aspects of our being. There is security forged in the sexual experience that can strengthen every aspect of the spousal relationship. It is far more than the high that comes from the adrenaline rush of looking for new sexual stimulation. It is truly a reflection of God's love for us, a sacrament at the core. It is time for our children to hear us talking about sex in these terms, not just hear us labeling body parts.

Sex is a beautiful, God-given gift that is designed to enhance our emotional and spiritual functioning. Unfortunately, many couples—even those in the church—settle for the cheap thrill of sexual pleasure in their marriages, never experiencing the full-ness of the gift that they have been given. Fear, bad previous sexual experiences, resentment in the marriage, previous physi-cal, sexual, or emotional abuse, and other things cause self-focus and an unwillingness to know and be known fully in the mar-riage relationship. This process of disconnecting from intimacy has far-reaching spiritual and relational consequences, as we will see in chapter eight. It also has implications for how our children grow to understand the relationship between sex and intimacy. Unfortunately, our self-protection leaves the very souls we are charged with protecting prone to injury.

Why Talk about Sex?

"If this is how I am designed, won't I just understand this once I am married?" This question carries with it powerful infer-ences. The question implies that there is no need to understand human sexuality until our biology kicks into gear and we have an appropriate outlet for our sexual urges. Most parents might actually prefer it that way, but it is not right thinking. The leg-acy of the sexual revolution in America is "sex anytime I want, however I want, with whomever I want, and as much as I want it"—while the legacy of silence within the church shrouds sex in secrecy and shame. Talk about dissonance. Our children are primed and ready for sexual activity around age twelve, and the average age of marriage in our culture is 28.7 years for men and 26.5 years for women.[4] Kids who have grown up in church have had a steady exposure to sexualized content—but no place to talk about it! How will your child fill those years between puberty and marriage? What are you doing to help him or her grow?

By and large, we avoid talking about sex as Christians. Per-haps one of your parents had "the talk" with you. If so, you may be a step ahead of the game as a parent, depending on how that experience went and the quality of content that was provided to you. That you are reading this book suggests your experience left a few stones unturned. If that's the case, you're in good company. The story I hear most frequently about "the talk" sounds something like this:

[Dad and son driving in the car]

Dad (dripping with sweat) to son: "Son, sex is a serious thing. Don't do it until you get married. Do you have any questions?"

Son (shaking head vigorously) to dad: "Nope." Son is thinking, *Are you kidding me? I'll never ask you anything about sex. Gross!*

Dad (with deep sigh of relief) to son: "Great talk. If you ever have any questions, let me know. Let's go get a pizza." Dad is thinking, *Phew! Glad to have that over! I hope he never asks questions. That would be awkward.*

Son to dad: "Sounds good. I'm starving." Son is thinking *I'm so glad he didn't ask any questions. If he only knew!*

As you can see, if this is the experience in the average American home, there is work to do. In our Christian homes, *if* we even have "the talk," it often carries with it implicit messages about our goodness or badness. Don't have sex, and you're a good boy or girl, because only bad boys and girls have sex.[5] This kind of logic can negatively impact your kids on their honeymoon.

Silence about the topic can also create a cloud of shame that can be difficult to shake as teenagers enter adulthood. Thus, there's a need for a better framework to assist us in talking with our kids about sex. It is critical that we approach "the conversation" very intentionally with a Christ-focused model, a model that does not prime our children for toxic shame as they launch into young adulthood. As a counselor I have seen this shame carry into the marriage relationship, and the consequences are steep.

Another reason to talk to our kids about sex is its seductive draw, which can ensnare them before anyone realizes it. We can shed some light on the pervasiveness of sexual behavior among our children's peer group in our culture if we look at the statistics on pornography. Pornography sites intentionally target the e-mails of twelve- to twenty-five-year-olds and advertise in many online gaming sites, because they know where young adults spend time. They are trolling for our kids' business. Pornography Web sites are frequented the most between the hours of 3 P.M. and 6 P.M., with the main demographic being adolescents.[6] Do you know what is happening in your home or what is occurring where your children hang out between those hours? Even if your kids are not in that age range, you may want to begin talking with them about what is safe and healthy regarding their online behaviors. Chapter five explores the sexual behaviors of "generation 'sext.'"

Accidental exposure is one of the primary culprits that introduces young children to porn. The business of pornography looks very similar to an addiction to pornography: it consumes incessantly without thought to the collateral damage being done to those unfortunate enough to cross its path. Do you have a blocking or filter system on your computer, such as Covenant Eyes? If not, it's time to invest in one, not because you can't trust your children but because you can't trust the people who are waging war against the spiritual, emotional, and sexual health of your children. This look into pornography use among teens suggests that the need to talk about sex more openly and directly is at an all-time high as well.

Cultural Shifts

Chances are that you fall into one of two camps: those who have had an awkward sex talk with your children, and those who have had no talk to this point. Hopefully the fact that you're

31

reading this book means that a conversation beyond the stereo-typical one described previously will be taking place soon. Perhaps you've already had "the talk" and picked up this book to gain a little more information on healthy sexuality. Whatever the case, my hope is that you will learn new and empowering information you can use to steward your child's sexuality well.

Even though "the talk" may be an awkward conversation for both you and your kids, the fact is that not educating them leaves them unequipped to navigate the social pressures awaiting them at school, on the Internet, in the locker room, on their cell phones, and elsewhere. Sex is everywhere, as we mentioned earlier. The daily messages that bombard all of us create dangerous and disturbing beliefs about sex that distort our perceptions and fuel our appetites for sexual gratification, especially if conversation about those messages and the sex they imply are not happening. As we become more desensitized to sex as a culture, those practices that have historically fallen outside the norm slowly become mainstream. A great example is pornography.

What used to be purchased in seedy motel rooms and gas stations is now readily available in your home on cable television and the Internet. Perhaps the most accurate description of life in this modern age of technology is this: cultural shift is happening. This ongoing cultural shift means a greater number of people are viewing pornography, many of whom believe there are no negative consequences for their behavior. This shift is not isolated to pornography. Sexual attitudes have shifted. Sexual practices have shifted. Sexual norms have shifted. Sexual preferences have shifted. Our children are not growing up in the same world we grew up in, and we must recognize that. We must prepare them to navigate these changes or be swept away by the power of their influence.

In light of these cultural shifts that have taken place, "the talk" should really be renamed "the conversation," because not everything about human sexuality can be fully discussed in one sitting. As their brains and bodies change, so does our children's ability to understand what sex is, how it functions, how their bodies work, and who God is in the mix of it all. Regardless of where it begins, "the conversation" is something that is critical to their healthy sexual development. As parents, you can better help your kids understand all these processes of change as they occur by being accurately informed yourself.

That is where this book comes in. It is up to you to start "the conversation." Just go for it! Otherwise the sound awaiting your children as they experience these changes in their bodies and in our culture will be the clicking and clacking of Google searches and sent "sext" messages.

Where Does It Start?

Okay, so you're geared up to answer the big question "What is sex?" And you've prepared yourself to enter into "the conversation" and forever alter the life of your child with some of the things you'll say. At this point you're probably asking yourself, *How do I talk about sex? I've always assumed that it's a secret, it's embarrassing, it's dirty, and it's inappropriate to talk about.* If that's the case, you're not alone. You'll need to shift your thinking quickly, though. As we'll see in the chapter titled "Generation 'Sext,'" sex is being talked about and explored *a lot.* As a parent, you'll need either to join "the conversation" or get left behind.

As funny as it may sound, even the secular world is uncomfortable actually talking about sex—perhaps not about the act itself but certainly about the essence of it. It's impossible to talk about sex without also addressing intimacy. Even when movies and magazine articles avoid talking about intimacy, they're still sending messages about it—mainly messages like "You can have sex without having intimacy" or even worse, "Sex *is* intimacy."

Intimacy is something that most folks in our culture are uncomfortable with. Have you gazed longingly into the eyes of your spouse recently? I didn't think so. Like eating broccoli or exercising, we dislike what's best for us. Next time you're in a social setting, sit back and observe. We don't like to be touched. We would rather text than talk on the phone. We spread out so we're not sitting right next to anyone—even at church. Our kids walk around with their eyes down, wearing ear buds or headphones with iPods or smartphones transporting them to some internal la-la land so they don't have to engage the world. We avoid contact at all costs in our culture, and in doing so, we become uncomfortable and unfamiliar with the intimacy that keeps us connected. It's no wonder our culture struggles with inappropriate sexual behaviors on such a global scale—we don't know how to relate to one another any other way.

Intimacy—meaning spiritual, emotional, *and* physical aspects of relational closeness—is good for us and is how our bodies are designed to operate. We usually hear the term *intimate* only to describe a sexual relationship. "We were *intimate* last night" becomes a euphemism for having sex. Even Christian couples who have been married for ten, twenty, or thirty years have likely only barely tasted intimacy in its fullness. We've been shaped by the subtle shifts in culture that define connection in sexual terms, while spiritual and emotional facets of our marriages have gone untended for years.

If you don't believe me, here's a little quiz: Men, when was the last time you touched your wife in a meaningful way without expecting it to lead to sex? Women, when is the last time you remember being touched and felt the freedom that the touch was not indicative of your husband's hunger for intercourse? For us to talk with our kids openly and honestly about sex and intimacy, we must first begin by engaging in these conversations in our marriages.

As we have seen, our culture has a tendency to dress up and sophisticate sexual acts, labeling them *intimacy* and allowing them to serve as a cheap replacement for the real thing. Sexualized *intimacy* does a great disservice to how we understand and engage in human relationships. If intimacy is sexual, then everything is sexual. And when everything is sexual, that's a problem. If everything is sexual, we do two things: (1) we move toward experiences that give us sexual pleasure, and (2) we move away from things that hold our sexual urges in check, such as community, prayer, and accountability.

Talking about sex has to involve talking about the act of sex more fully than we normally do, meaning we have to talk about more than body parts. It is important that we include a definition for intimacy that our kids can relate to and understand as we discuss sexuality. Any part of "the conversation" that is only about body parts and their functions is really a primitive attempt at "the talk" and falls short of its full potential, although it's better than nothing (usually). Because sex is about more than simple body parts and their functions, "the conversation" must reflect the thoughts, emotions, and spiritual dynamics that comprise the whole of who we are as sexual beings. Your timing, openness, and honesty are critical in driving "the conversation" toward a healthy end.

As stated previously, one reason you may not have had the talk with your kids is what you uncovered in chapter one. Perhaps while growing up you received signals that sex is not okay to talk about. You might have been shut down when you tried to ask a question or were caught in some sexual exploration behavior that was never properly discussed. You may still be able to feel the shame of that moment as you reflect. There are many reasons this conversation may not have taken place yet, the majority of which tie directly back to our own experiences and corresponding dis-comfort with sexuality.

Perhaps you learned about sex through movies, magazines, or personal experience when you were young rather than from your mother or father. Regardless, it is impossible to facilitate an hon-est and meaningful conversation about intimacy without much practice at actually *being* intimate. More than just benefitting your kids as they live in an increasingly sexual world, perhaps you, too, can have a corrective experience in giving your children the gift of the real sex education you never got—an honest, bib-lical, developmentally appropriate conversation about sex. This book is designed to serve as a guide so that you are informed in making "the conversation" a meaningful, educational, and per-haps even tolerable experience for your children.

Because intimacy is so important in living healthful emotion-al, spiritual, and sexual lives, chapter six is dedicated solely to attachment. This content serves as a guide for establishing inti-macy across the lifespan. You might even pick up a thing or two for your marriage as you read. For right now you can use this definition of intimacy with your kids: "the fullness of closeness in a significant life relationship that grows us into our greatest potential in all parts of our lives." We can be intimate with our friends, intimate with our siblings, intimate with our parents and grandparents, and intimate with Christ. When intimacy is sexu-alized, however, we're left disconnected from the very relation-ships that are meant to blossom our gifts and talents. Outside the context of the marriage relationship, sex is simply a tool used to take power, experience pleasure, and objectify people; in no way does it help us get closer to become the best people we are called to be or closer to the God we serve. If your experience of intimacy has been hurtful, neglectful, traumatic, or downright absent, or if you have struggled with exploring sexual behaviors like masturbation or intercourse, take heart. The beginnings of healthy connection are just one conversation away.

Sex Talks

You will find that the information about human sexuality detailed in this book has been intentionally divided into three sections: "Sex: Myths and Messages," "Sex: Technology, Biology, and Intimacy," and "The Finer Points: STARTing 'the Conversation.'" Within each section you will find the necessary information to dialogue with your children about sexual health and development, including biological, emotional, and spiritual aspects. Regardless of your children's ages, your relationship will grow and deepen by entering into "the conversation."

three

DON JUAN,
CONQUISTADOR

When it comes to love and romance, American men are completely lost. The movie *Hitch* brilliantly depicts the innocence of this male confusion regarding the female species. Mostly well-meaning, many men simply get in their own way when it comes to facilitating the authentic relationship they are looking for with a woman. But there are also those who take a very different view of women, seeing them as mere notches in the belt of sexual prowess. Much of the framework for under-standing male sexuality centers on the notion of conquest. Like Christopher Columbus arriving on the shores of North America and planting a flag of ownership, men believe that their sexual exploits give them credibility and identity.

If the term *conquest* is not disturbing enough in its own right, when we look a bit deeper into the definition, we see the same root used as in "conquer," or "to gain or acquire by force of arms; to subjugate," according to Merriam-Webster. The 1960s antiwar slogan "Make love, not war" has become "The war between the lovers," each party trying to take something from the other.

Biblically, we see that love is something that can be given but not taken. Unfortunately, this notion of conquest plays itself out in the lives of many Bible-believing men and husbands. When conquest is the defining attribute for male approaches to sexual encounter, the emotional and spiritual connection that we are created for cannot be felt. This cultural misunderstanding fuels the sexual myths that males operate with.

Boys Will Be Boys

If you are a man, everywhere you turn there are messages being communicated to you about sex. From the magazine rack at the grocery store to online advertisements, these messages inundate the lives of young men, subtly shaping their ideas and expectations about sex. It is nearly impossible to check your e-mail or buy a pack of gum without being confronted by some myth about male sexuality. At the heart of this cultural rampage against healthy male sexuality are five popular myths that falsely shape the perspective of young men about what sex truly is.

The most tragic belief that we hold as a culture about male sexuality is that "boys will be boys." The notion that we are wired to act like juveniles across the lifespan, especially in the area of sexual behavior, is fatalism (life happens beyond our influence to change it) at its finest. This belief is best articulated as "We have no power over our behaviors, sexual or otherwise, so we give into them until perversion becomes normative." It is fascinating how quickly fatalism becomes *hedonism,* which is considering pleasure as the highest virtue. The following myths about male sexuality all tie into this notion that pleasure is the highest good and thus the most important thing to pursue.

Five Common Myths about Male Sexuality

Myth #1: *Men think about sex every seven seconds.* While men have been shown to think about sex on a more regular basis than women, the idea that men think about sex every seven seconds is difficult to believe. As humans we take about one breath every seven seconds. To think that a man has as many thoughts about sex per day as breaths—approximately eight thousand—is fundamentally untrue. Sociologist Edward Laumann and his colleagues found in a 1994 study that men think about sex anywhere from a few times a day down to a few times per month.[1] While we can assume this frequency has increased with the sexualization of culture in the past twenty years, it is highly doubtful that the average man thinks about sex every seven seconds. The average teenager? Now that's a different story.

Myth #2: *Men are always ready for sex.* Building on the previous myth, it would make sense that if men thought about sex every seven seconds, they would always be ready for a sexual encounter. While this might be a more true statement for younger men, the fact is that many variables contribute to a man's ability and willingness to engage his spouse sexually, regardless of age. Fatigue, stress, and depression are just a few of the dynamics that can limit the male libido. One reason we tend to believe this myth is that men tend to move toward sexual contact when their cortisol—the stress hormone—levels increase, whereas women tend to move away from sexual contact when their cortisol levels rise.

In our overstressed culture, the sexual disconnect experienced in many marriages is directly linked to this physiological principle. More important, even when a man is ready for sex, his biblical responsibility is to sacrifice his own desires for the good of his spouse. That is a message you won't find in Hollywood.

Myth #3: *Men always initiate sex.* This might be the myth with the most grounding in reality. While men do not *always* initiate sex, many married people I have worked with struggle with this pattern of behavior. Unfortunately, many men do not know how to pursue their wives emotionally and spiritually and instead rely on their grabby hands to demonstrate their affection. Nonsexual touch in the marriage relationship is critical in creating a safe and secure environment where intimacy can blossom. Men are more likely to initiate sex, but men also want to be desired. They long to be sought after and pursued by their wives. They long to be held and nurtured but often do not have the courage to ask. When these emotional needs are stifled through rejection and shame, especially during later childhood and adolescence, the seeds of more dangerous myths such as objectification, power, and intensity are sown. Fathers, let your sons see you hold your wife tenderly and pursue her emotionally. Mothers, let your sons see you encourage and validate your husband.

Myth #4: *Single men have better sex than married men.*[2] Apparently the grass *is* always greener on the other side. Many of the young bachelors I have counseled eagerly await finding their true love and having sex. Their struggles with pornography and promiscuity leave them desiring much more from a relationship. Culture idolizes the lone-wolf bachelor who is out on the prowl at clubs and raves, hunting his prey and demonstrating his sexual prowess. Our collective fantasy about these men is that they are out having as much sex as they want with the most attractive women. We believe them to have the best of all worlds: the freedom to do whatever they please and the finances to do it. Many of the difficulties faced by the married men I have counseled stem from trying to emulate this life. Like Dorothy seeing behind the curtain, the truth reveals a particular disappointment and shock. There is no wizard. As it turns out, married men report having more sex and better sex than their single counterparts.

Myth #5: *Sex ends with physical pleasure.* For the man who approaches sex as a conquest, this myth operates as a reality in his delusional way of life. He has taken what he wants, namely pleasure, and subsequently disengages from physical contact. In one-night stands, often the social contact ends at the same time the physical contact does. Once the pleasure is gone, so too is the physical contact. Each of these examples sheds light on the broken understanding of healthy sex that we have in our culture. On a physiological level, physical pleasure serves as a *beginning* rather than an ending. Changes in hormones such as oxytocin, which enables trust and connection to grow, and vasopressin, which enhances partner preference and pair-bonding, are released.[3] When we roll over, leave the room, or move away from physical, emotional, and spiritual contact with our spouses following sex, we incapacitate our body's God-given ability to deepen intimacy. It is our discomfort with vulnerability that often drives this process. We move away from the very space that God has given us to experience acceptance, comfort, and safety in relationship.

Back to Reality

I feel great pain and sadness for the boys and young men who have to grow up in this hypersexual culture. These messages have a powerful draw and create the belief that sex is the most important aspect of the human experience. I am sure that my parents thought the same thing, as did their parents before them, so there is some universality to this feeling. It comes with the territory of parenting.

With that being said, most days it seems as if today's youth have no escape or reprieve from the tsunami of sexualized messages, images, and innuendos that crash down on them, assaulting their senses and shaping their minds toward a more permissive understanding of human sexuality. Sex is truly everywhere in our children's world.

I was with my family at the mall over the Christmas holiday while on vacation in Dallas when the full reality of this truth smacked me square between the eyes. As we walked into the mall, we observed a pet adoption agency conducting a Christmas pet drive, trying to get parents like me to fall in love with an adorable little kitten or playful puppy to take home and put under the Christmas tree. As my family looked at these cute and cuddly animals, my older son heard Justin Bieber playing over the speakers and began to investigate the source of the music. You have to understand that my son idolized Justin Bieber at the time—right up until we introduced him to a steady diet of TobyMac—and would dance like a madman every time he heard these songs. He did not have to go far before I saw him stop dead in his tracks.

I hurried around the corner after him and, as my eyes found the source of the music, I understood why his jaw was on the floor. He had stumbled upon a perfect cocktail of audiovisual pleasure: a sixteen-by-twenty-foot screen playing a recorded Justin Bieber concert, which conveniently portrayed Victoria's Secret models walking down the runway in skimpy lingerie. He was in awe. His little eyes did their best to drink in every last drop of the visual ambrosia before him.

I took stock of the situation. Here was an innocent five-year-old little boy who was mesmerized by beautiful, nearly naked women with perfectly toned and proportioned bodies who were moving in perfect harmony with the beat that was his favorite musician's catchy tune. I can only imagine the associations that were made in his inquisitive brain that day at the mall. Between the music and the images he took in, he is sure to have made the connection between the music and beauty, as well as desire to be associated with both. Five-year-old minds are much more in tune with the world than we might think. As I gathered myself, the importance of the moment crept through the relief, and I understood that this was a powerful teaching moment for both of us. Rather than allowing my fears to transform into an overtly shaming moment for my son, or allowing the boys-will-be-boys mentality to simply dismiss the experience altogether, I calmly reached for his hand. "It's time to go," I said, and he walked with me to the door of the mall. Once outside, I knelt down beside him and asked him what he had seen on the screen inside.

"Those are some pretty women, Daddy," he whispered.

"They are not as pretty as your mama, buddy," I replied. "But you're right—they *are* pretty."

I went on to explain to him that his favorite musician was simply doing advertising and that the world of advertising and the real world are two different things. Advertising creates a world that is make-believe, full of sights and sounds designed to make you feel as if you're not good enough and will never be good enough unless you buy what they're selling. What they're selling is more than underwear—it's a way of thinking about oneself and about girls. It takes you out of the world of actual relationships and facts and into a world of fantasies and distortions.

While he's not yet old enough to understand the concept of objectification, he had his first experience with it there in the mall in Dallas—as well as the first of many conversations he will hear from me about the role of culture in teaching us to devalue women rather than valuing them for who they are as mothers, spouses, and daughters. He will hear the fact that as real men we do not stand for this.

Sexual Dis-funk-tion: Three Distortions of Male Sexuality

Times are changing. For you and me, sex talks with our children will have to center more specifically on addressing the myths and messages foisted upon them by our culture. The act of stewarding our children's sexuality extends far beyond informing them of their body parts and the corresponding uses. This educational process is still necessary—but ultimately insufficient. Sex is more than body parts fulfilling their intended use. This conversation must be defined by filling the emotional and spiritual spaces in our children's lives with messages that counteract the half-truths found in abundance in our culture. Our children are loved; they are prized; they are cherished; they are accepted. In a time when their lives are being invaded with distorted messages about what it means to be a man, our boys need fathers and male role models who stand on solid biblical principles with messages about true and healthy masculinity.

Objectification

The underlying myths about sexuality that young boys are first exposed to center around this notion of *objectification*. Objectification is best defined as viewing another for the benefit they provide to me, regardless of the cost to them. With the sexualization of our culture, younger and younger children believe the message that other people exist for their own gratification, sexual or otherwise.

Toddlers are quick to pick up on the concept of *mine*. The news has been full of stories in recent years of students who engage in sexual relationships with their older teachers, students who have committed suicide following a sex tape or images being released in the school of their performing sexual acts, and students who begin to perpetrate sexual offenses against younger children. The central theme in these stories has to do with the blatant objectification of the other as an "it." "*It* is mine"—a thing to be enjoyed for a while and then discarded, regardless of the consequences it brings. At the center of this myth is the pornography industry.

Pornographic films require little imagination, little artistry, and even less acting ability. Shallow and empty, they are devoid of any meaningful human interaction and instead focus more explicitly and intensely on the body parts performing sexual acts. There is little kissing, little eye contact, and zero caressing or comforting touch. It is a hollow act that is designed to elicit a fantasy about what sex *should* be like or *could* be like.

This first component of objectification happens when we believe that sexual acts and our sex organs exist independently from the rest of our bodies. This dualistic thinking severs the connection between our physical selves and our emotional and spiritual selves. Individuals who struggle with pornography addiction get lost in simply seeing and responding to the parts of the body that are presented. They escape into a fantasy where their body is experiencing the acts taking place on screen—a fantasy that reality cannot compete with.

This fantasy and disconnection of the parts of themselves is the only way one can explain the vast quantities of pornography that center on the theme of hurting, humiliating, or injuring another. The person experiencing these painful physical and emotional acts is not a person in the eyes of the consumer but a thing, an object to be devoured and then discarded, like an empty carcass, never to be thought of again. And we wonder why zombies are all the rage for this generation.

Take an example that is largely commonplace among the parents of the millennial generation that I have worked with. Their exposure to sexual content is not so different from my very own. At the age of eight or nine I went with my parents and siblings to a family gathering over Labor Day weekend. We went to the lake, swam in the pool, sang around the campfire, and then the adults stayed up late playing games. Being the middle of three children, I often found myself somewhere in between stages.

In this instance, my younger sister had already been put to bed and my older brother was actively engaged in card-playing with our extended family. On this particular night, I was sitting on the couch, tired and bored, looking for something to do. I perused the selection of magazines available on the coffee table in front of me. Much to my delight, I read a title that sounded intriguing to my young mind. *That must be filled with all sorts of wonderful ideas for games and activities that we can do tomorrow,* I thought. Innocently, I opened *Playboy* and began to turn through the pages.

Much to my wonderment I encountered a lot more than ideas for the next day's outdoor adventures. Page after page held the promise of more adrenaline as my conscience screamed, "Warning! Warning!" with every picture I absorbed.

At some point, someone looked up from the card table and said, "Oh, my—look what Todd is reading!" With my conscience smugly reminding me that it had "told me so," I faced the inquisition about why I had picked up the magazine, what I had seen, and if I were telling the truth. As you can guess, my answers were "I was looking for things to do tomorrow," "I didn't see anything," and "Yes, I'm telling the truth." Well, at least I told the truth to one of those questions.

On the inside I was fearful and ashamed, not just for having seen what I had seen but also for lying about it to protect myself. That experience of fear, shame, and arousal set a template in my life that took many years to work through. I had learned the art of *objectifying.*

I had learned that I didn't need to connect with someone to feel the feelings I had in my body. I had learned that there were things I could see that made me feel one sensation emotionally (shame) and another physically (arousal). The physical sensation of pleasure seemingly always outweighs any emotional consequences. This template, forged in the fear and shame of that experience, is the story of a generation.

Objectifying, then, can be seen as a process that involves depersonalizing the other as a thing, viewing the person simply as body parts that exist for our pleasure, waiting to be consumed and then discarded. In this mind-set, nakedness is seen as an opportunity for pleasure rather than a person to share intimacy with.

It would be a mistake for us to think that objectification is a purely sexual mind-set. Video games embed the belief that there are no consequences for our decisions. We can hit "reset" anytime we want. Movies depict killing as simple as sneezing—and just about as common. We can kill, maim, and destroy with little thought. While this distorted belief about human sexuality for males is disturbing, what is more disturbing is what emerges from this mind-set, namely, that sex is about *having* power by *taking* power from another. Once again, pornography is the primary driving force of this now-engrained male belief system.

Power

It is impossible to talk about sex without also talking about power. Each person inevitably has something the other person desires, and he or she will either share with one another, or one will take from the other.

Unhealthy sexual relationships remind me of chimpanzees at the zoo. They steal with reckless abandon, never pausing to understand one another's needs or desires. How often do we fall prey to the same way of relating in our marriages? In healthy situations, communication and negotiation of how the needs of both parties will be met serve to create balance. Everybody wins. In unhealthy situations, the desire of one trumps the desire or willingness of the other. Individual desire, unchecked, supersedes the good of the relationship. Rather than power being shared, it is hoarded and used selfishly.

Sex in American culture is used as a means of power on many fronts. From rape to marketing exploits and everything in between, we see sex used as a tool for obtaining influence, status, money, and possessions—all markers of power. This statement was certainly true before Madonna entered pop culture in the early 1980s; however, the impact she has had on American culture in how we think about, talk about, see, and have sex is undeniable.

While it might be easy to assume that this issue originated and exists solely in the secular world, as Christians we must take a hard look at how we have defined sexuality across the years. Many of the baby boomers who have come through the door of my clinical practice use a similar biblical term to describe sex in their marriages—*birthright*.

Their notion is that the pleasure, release, and escape provided by sex in the marriage is theirs by biblical mandate. "We are married, so her body is mine." That sounds eerily similar to objectification in my book. Whenever I want it, however I want it, as much as I want it. It is impossible to separate objectification from power. When we objectify another, we use him or her as a means to our personal end, even if it is only in our mind, as Christ discusses in Matthew 5:28. Rather than embodying the selflessness and sacrifice that we are called to in Ephesians 5, as men we have become takers in our sexualized culture—not the givers and pursuers we are created to be but takers who focus more on personal gratification than connection. Husband, are you addicted to your wife's body? If so, can you love her spiritually and emotionally in the way that you are called to? What messages are your sons and daughters perceiving when your love is more defined by *eros* than *agape*? Are you really willing to empty yourself for your wife as Christ did for the church? A generation of boys will be shaped by how you and I choose to answer these questions.

Our children's first messages about sex are what they see taking place—or not taking place—in the marriage relationship. Many parents fear their children walking into the bedroom and catching them in the act. Unfortunately, it is the nonsexual messages that have a more profound influence on how our children come to understand relationship—and by extension—sex.

Men, the lack of emotional engagement and the unwillingness to help with dishes and laundry speak volumes. The side remarks of "It's been seventy-two hours—where's my lovin'?" do not go unnoticed. We fear the thing that will likely never occur and miss the elephant standing in the room beside us.

As Christians, the distorted belief of power is found in the most unexpected of places: our homes. If you encourage your children but not your wife, you make yourself a hypocrite in their eyes. If you talk at dinner with your kids about their day and don't acknowledge your spouse at the table, you make yourself a hypocrite in their eyes. If this principle resonates with you, the chapter on attachment will be of particular interest to you.

Intensity

When objectification and power become defining beliefs about sex, it is inevitable to perceive the need for high-intensity sexual experiences. In many respects, men graduate into this belief about the need for sex to be intense after long histories of struggling with faulty beliefs about objectification and power. In many respects, intense sex is the proverbial dangling carrot.

Regardless of how intense our experience might be, the messages we receive from countless magazines from *Cosmopolitan* to *Maxim* and everything in between suggest that there is a more intense high that can be experienced, some new technique to be implemented, or some new forbidden pleasure that can be discovered. Beneath the glossy cover and attractive language is an emptiness that will never be satisfied.

The message communicated by these articles is based on a deficit model. We are fundamentally lacking or incomplete, while everyone who participates in the suggested behavior is satisfied and content. "You are not good enough unless . . ." The same pressure that we help our children negotiate during middle school with profound logical insights such as "If everyone were jumping off a bridge, would you?" is the same pressure that we are falling victim to in our own lives and marriages. Certain sexual experiences open the door to an intensity that is difficult to match without ingesting a powerful stimulant. In an effort to feel normal, we are the ones jumping off the proverbial bridge, and our children are following suit.

Three terms to keep in mind when thinking about intensity are adrenaline, novelty, and visual stimulation. *Adrenaline* is the neurotransmitter of the sympathetic nervous system.[4] Think about the last time you were on a roller coaster, at a scary movie, or saw the flashing of red-and-blue lights in your rearview mirror. Chances are that you had a physical reaction to that experience, such as your heart racing, your blood-pressure spiking, and all your senses heightening. Adrenaline intensifies our experience, because it pulls us into more primitive brain structures such as the amygdala—the fear center of the brain.

The amygdala, or fear center of the brain, focuses predominantly on our individual survival instincts of fight, flight, and freeze; it is not an altruistic structure. Sexually, adrenaline intensifies the experience of pleasure at the expense of a sense of connection.

In addition to adrenaline, *novelty* is an important ingredient in the intensity process. Think back to the first time you experienced something new. Assuming it wasn't a terrible experience of some sort, the novelty of it enhanced the positive experience. In the sexual addiction treatment that I provide, novelty hijacks the brain. The obsessive need for new and deviant stimulation drives folks to deeper and darker places of the Internet. Eventually, some people end up at massage parlors and brothels, paying for more novel experiences to increase the high of the sexual experience.

Before we completely throw novelty under the bus, it is important to acknowledge that novelty in and of itself is not an overtly negative dynamic. When used appropriately, novelty—such as a vacation—can enhance the sexual experience in the relationship and keep the embers of physical passion burning.

Last, intensity is driven by *visual stimulation*. Pornography entails this dynamic as the receiver is *watching* the act take place. When the focus of attention is watching sex happen rather than experiencing the other with whom love is being made, "Houston, we have a problem."

Raising sexually healthy sons will involve dispelling these myths and distorted beliefs at some point. As fathers, our greatest influence is found in letting our sons see healthy relationship lived out from an early age, educating them along the way as they grow and develop. Their lives are already inundated with sexual messages and materials; they need a role model who can help them navigate the choppy waters of childhood and adolescence. The lingering question remains for us as fathers: are you willing to become this man for your kids?

four
PRINCESS

As a culture, we all want our daughters to be princesses who are sweet, compassionate, and pure. We want them to follow the rules and make intelligent choices. There is no other way to explain the reality television phenomenon known as *Toddlers and Tiaras*. The story of Rapunzel provides some insight into this collective belief system in that many parents want to keep their daughter safe and pure, locked away in a proverbial tower until the right prince comes along and sweeps her off of her feet. In fact, Disney recently produced a movie about this exact dynamic, with a very twenty-first-century twist.

In *Tangled*, the caregiver is portrayed as selfish and evil for trying to squelch love rather than letting it blossom. In this portrayal, children witness the injustice and oppression of parental values and decisions, creating an implicit tension between parents and children regarding personal values. Basically you are being told as a parent that you are wrong for trying to raise your children with values different from what popular culture deems permissible. Didn't catch that when you watched it? Watch it again.

It is interesting that Disney validates the myth of objectification we saw in the last chapter but defends its stance with the free-will argument. "It's okay to be seen and treated as an object as long as you get to choose who uses you" is the meta-message in many of their films over the past three decades. Young girls everywhere have bought in—hook, line, and sinker.

I've never been a fifteen-year-old girl, but from my understanding, this idea of "love" is a common parent-child conflict that begins sometime during puberty. As the dating years begin, there is a delicate balance to be negotiated in the process of development—one that our children sometimes simply don't see our side of. If we use the *Tangled* example, we know that inside the tower our daughters are safe and loved, but outside the tower unrealistic expectations and implicit sexual pressures shape their beliefs about themselves, others, and the world around them. While we cannot keep them locked away in the tower forever, we can equip them to take ownership for the balance, safety, and health that the tower provides. Facilitating secure attachment, discussed in detail in chapter seven, is essential in equipping our daughters to stay healthy sexually, spiritually, and emotionally as they develop and launch into society.

Let me start by saying this: you are right. You are right to trust your instincts. You are right to be worried for your daughter. The world has changed drastically. Messages about sex target our kids with a savvy brilliance seen in few other arenas. For example, Victoria's Secret has been very successful with their "Pink" slogan that is written across the back of panties, shorts, and sweatpants worldwide. Take one trip through the mall, and you will find that adolescents and young women alike flaunt their bodies in garments with this term intentionally located on one particular region of their bodies.

While the clothing might not seem harmful in its own right, this idea of sexualizing clothing is just the tip of the iceberg when it comes to considering *how* we think about sex. Specifically, it signifies a shift in how young girls are thinking about themselves, exploring sexuality at younger ages.

I hate to badger, but have you *seen* a Victoria's Secret ad recently? Objectification barely begins to describe it. The desire for surgical procedures among teenagers—and not out of medical necessity—are commonplace now. Young women are trying to live up to a standard that is unattainable without surgery and airbrushes.

Just to be clear, I am not suggesting that you're bad parent if your daughter wears these clothes. I *am* suggesting that we need to open the lines of communication with our kids about the messages being communicated by the clothing they wear—or don't wear, as the case may be. This marketing strategy is sexual innuendo at its finest, innocently introduced by us into their wardrobes in an attempt to "keep up with the Joneses."

Parents, it's time for us to wake up and smell the coffee. When it comes to healthy sexuality, the Joneses, it turns out, are not worth keeping up with. Since the sexual revolution, the pressure on women to be highly sexual has increased, leaving today's young women in tremendous confusion about who they really are: your sweet innocent daughter or some sexual object that chooses its owner.

Three Common Myths about Female Sexuality

Myth #1: *Sex is not important to women.*[1] Nearly one hundred percent of the women I have provided therapy to across the years claim that this myth is an outright lie. When defined through the same lens of release and pleasure that men describe, the statement is very likely true. However, the function that sex serves in the relationship for these women is vastly different. Women report sex as a very important physical expression of love and affirmation in the relationship when it occurs as the climax of emotional closeness rather than a physical experience devoid of emotion. Sex is important to women in different ways than it is important to men, and most husbands I have met have difficulty understanding this.

I would suggest that most women have a stronger sense of healthy sexuality than most men. They incorporate kissing, talking, and caressing more intentionally into the sexual experience. When our understanding of sex develops into one of mutuality, nurturance, and communion, then we begin to understand the importance of sex to women, and sex actually becomes a source of connection in the relationship rather than a source of tension or division. Men, we have work to do in this area.

Myth #2: *Women desire sex less than men.* Building on the previous myth, the notion that women have less desire for sex is also fundamentally dependent on what we use as the benchmark for healthy sex drive. The myth for males involves hyperactive sexual desire—as demonstrated by the seven-second fallacy and the belief that men are ready for sex at any time. When we debunk these myths and operate from a more balanced understanding of sexual desire, we find that sex drive is roughly equivalent between males and females.

Once again, sex serves a different function for females than for males, so the expression of desire is very different. Women might be satisfied with sexual expression entailing an evening of kissing and cuddling. In a man's mind, the kissing and cuddling are the launch sequence for a much larger process. Sorry, guys, but the women have it right here. Sex is not always intercourse. Shocking, I know. Try it sometime. Give her a back rub and don't expect anything in return. If you are caring and nurturing only in an attempt to get sex, you are acting selfishly. At the very core, these two myths are driven by the faulty belief that sex is solely about pleasure rather than the fullness of intimacy that it is intended to be.

Myth #3: *When a woman says "no," she really means "yes."* This myth is by far the most disturbing cultural myth about female sexuality and has been birthed by the sense of objectification, power, and intensity that men in American culture use to define sex. Rape, molestation, and sex trafficking are societal tragedies that illustrate this myth, directly birthed or reinforced by the pornography industry. Most pornographic films contain sexually violent or degrading/dehumanizing themes.[2] Frequent pornography users have been found to score higher on acceptance of the rape myth, acceptance of violence against women, reported likelihood of committing rape and forced sex acts, and sexual callousness than those who watch infrequently or not at all.[3]

When Ted Bundy confessed that pornography played a role in his murder of twenty-eight women, American culture scoffed. However, study after study confirms that exposure to violent pornography inverts our sense of decency and humanity by having us believe that women who are raped, beaten, or killed either had it coming for their provocative style of dress or actually were enjoying being abused physically and sexually.[4]

"It is now conventional wisdom that there is overwhelming scientific evidence linking pornography with sexual violence." Lynne Segal wrote those words in 1990.[5] 1990! In the time that has passed, our level of global desensitization to violence against women persists. As a culture, we are a lot more like Bundy than we would like to believe.

Sexualization

Many of these myths have contributed to the premature development of exploratory sexuality among young teenagers and older children. Eager to emulate that which they have been exposed to and heard peers discussing for years, these students begin to explore sexual behaviors at younger and younger ages.

Chevonea Kendall-Bryan was thirteen when she fell sixty feet to the ground and died from the resulting head injuries. The fall was the result of a young man calling on her—a twisted twenty-first-century depiction of Romeo and Juliet. Rather than being drawn together in love, lust was the force that permeated the events leading up to her death. The young man had a video of Chevonea performing a sexual act on a friend of his, and he was pressuring her into providing him the same gratification. She threatened to jump if he did not delete the video. Then she slipped. While the cause of death was massive brain injury, the darker backdrop surrounding her death can be summed up in one word: *pornification.*

This tragic story depicts the brutal consequences of the sexualization of girls in Western cultures, with pornography as a driving force in the process. The American Psychological Association's Task Force on the Sexualization of Girls identifies four primary components to the process of sexualization.[6]

First, sexualization occurs when one's value or worth is defined solely by sexual appeal or behavior. This would suggest that our sexual organs define us more than our intangible qualities or person.

Second, there is an overemphasis on meeting a physically attractive standard to be considered sexy. As we have seen with the advent of plastic surgery, this standard is physically unattainable without the "assistance" of physical modifications.

Third, a person who is being sexualized is being sexually objectified, or being seen as simply a means to an end.

Fourth, sexualization involves sexual activity being forced on or expected by a person without consent.

The disturbing story of Chevonea Kendall-Bryan sheds light on the tangled web of sexualization we have created in Western cultures. From 2002 to 2008, the number of teenage girls who had sex with more than one partner doubled.[7] As the sexual trends explored in chapter five suggest, this sexualization process has opened a Pandora's Box for generation "sext." The emotional, cognitive, sexual, and societal consequences stemming from the sexualization of girls and young women reinforce the distorted beliefs about male sexuality—and also create a number of distorted beliefs about female sexuality.

Little White Lies: Three Distortions of Female Sexuality

Love and acceptance. For some women, sex is not so much an expression of intimacy as it is a tool to fill their longing for love and acceptance. Our cultural aversion to touch exists at the heart of this distorted belief about sex. Nonsexual touch is critical to establishing healthy attachment relationships. These relationships serve as the foundation for our understanding of ourselves, our self-concept. We know who we are as a result of our experiences in relationship with those we love. In many ways, our attachment figures hold a mirror in front of us and give us the ability to observe ourselves. Through this process we are able to integrate certain attitudes, behaviors, and beliefs that resonate with us, and discard those that do not.

When girls do not receive the nonsexual touch and affirmation they need, they can become touch-starved. Not only are they starving for physical affirmation, but they are also starving for emotional and spiritual validation. In a culture where acting sexual gets you attention, these young ladies find the love and acceptance they are looking for via their sexuality. The physical act of sex may not even be engaged in during their teenage years, but the pattern of behavior they are establishing by pairing sexual cues with feeling loved and accepted will eventually cross the threshold once intercourse is explored. This dynamic is present in female sex and love addicts.[8]

Beauty. Similar to filling the void of love and acceptance experienced by so many young ladies, sex serves to squelch the whispers in their minds that they will never be beautiful. In a culture where airbrushed models set the standard for attractiveness, young women grow up feeling inferior to the expectation foisted upon them. Television, Hollywood, magazines, and now pornography depict sex as a gateway for beauty. The sexualization of young women drives this distorted belief in that younger and younger girls are emulating the cultural standard. They are too young to know that the "standard" is fictitious.

In the absence of messages about their beauty from parents and family, these girls turn to sex as a mechanism to feel beautiful. In their minds, the easiest way to feel beautiful is to be desired by as many potential sexual partners as possible. In generation sexy, beauty is only skin deep—or better yet, screen deep. The cries to be seen as beautiful emanating from these young women is deafening, and they are completely unaware that they are screaming.

Significance. The greatest wound that young women walk around with today is the feeling of insignificance. Whereas men express power through more dominant behaviors, women express power through this notion of significance. *I am seen. I am desired. People know who I am.* Marnie Ferree also states, "Culture portrays sex as a woman's ticket to getting almost anything she wants," and she is right.[9] To be significant is to have worth.

In the absence of a framework for understanding oneself as anything other than an object due to the pervasive objectification and sexualization they have experienced, young women fall prey to the lie that their worth is found in their ability to be sexually pleasing. It should come as no surprise that adult escort services generate eleven billion dollars yearly worldwide.[10]

Stewarding our daughters' sexuality is first and foremost about helping them understand who they are. These little white lies do not take root when there is a strong bond between a daughter and her parents. From this connection, a young woman is able to experience godly love and acceptance, to understand the scriptural essence of beauty, and to find significance in the depth of her emotional and spiritual connection with others rather than in the fleeting pleasures of sexuality. As parents of young women, our desire is to raise them to be defined by the noble qualities listed in Proverbs 31:10-31—

A wife of noble character who can find? She is worth far more than rubies. Her husband has full confidence in her and lacks nothing of value. She brings him good, not harm, all the days of her life. She selects wool and flax and works with eager hands. She is like the merchant ships, bringing her food from afar. She gets up while it is still night; she provides food for her family and portions for her female servants. She considers a field and buys it; out of her earnings she plants a vineyard. She sets about her work vigorously; her arms are strong for her tasks. She sees that her trading is profitable, and her lamp does not go out at night. In her hand she holds the distaff and grasps the spindle with her fingers. She opens her arms to the poor and extends her hands to the needy. When it snows, she has no fear for her household; for all of them are clothed in scarlet. She makes coverings for her bed; she is clothed in fine linen and purple. Her husband is respected at the city gate, where he takes his seat among the elders of the land. She makes linen garments and sells them, and supplies the merchants with sashes. She is clothed with strength and dignity; she can laugh at the days to come. She speaks with wisdom, and faithful instruction is on her tongue. She watches over the affairs of her household and does not eat the bread of idleness. Her children arise and call her blessed; her husband also, and he praises her: "Many women do noble things, but you surpass them all." Charm is deceptive, and beauty is fleeting; but a woman who fears the LORD is to be praised. Honor her for all that her hands have done, and let her works bring her praise at the city gate.

Section Two

SEX
TECHNOLOGY, BIOLOGY, AND INTIMACY

five

GENERATION "SEXT"

S ex and the American teenager is an ever-evolving concept. A variety of movements have emerged to address this issue, such as abstinence-based education, "safe-sex" approaches, and others. Teens are having intercourse less frequently than we typically believe, with only twenty-seven percent reporting to have had intercourse within the past three months.[1]

Unfortunately, condom use among sexually active individuals is relatively low as well, right at twenty-five percent.[2] This chapter is meant to bring to your attention relevant information so that you can get a realistic overview of sex in American culture, especially trends among adolescents, teenagers, and young adults. Get to know generation "sext."

Pornography

"Be careful, little eyes, what you see." Those seven words have never rung so true as in the ears of parents today. With the boom in technology that our culture has experienced over the past twenty years, the availability of pornographic images may be at an all-time high. It is big business. According to *The Social Costs of Pornography,* the United States accounts for about thirteen billion dollars of the ninety-seven billion dollars made worldwide each year in the pornography industry, and there are more than eleven thousand pornographic films shot in the United States each year—or a little more than thirty per day.[3] To put that in perspective, Hollywood produces about four hundred films in a good year, or a little more than one per day.

The same technological mediums that have the ability to facilitate human connection and interaction for people from across the globe have been perverted into warehouses of sexually explicit materials and voyeuristic playgrounds. You might assume that this is a problem just for adolescent and young adult males; if you do, you are wrong. Pornography use among young women is at an all-time high.[4]

This influence is being seen in the video game world and other parts of the worldwide web as well. A study in Britain suggests that the average child watching cartoons on YouTube is just three clicks away from explicit content. Claire Lilley of Britain's National Society for the Prevention of Cruelty to Children states that we are "facing an e-safety time bomb."[5] Given their technological literacy, it is nearly impossible for an eleven-year-old child to avoid. The following are the top ten statistics that parents need to be aware of regarding teens and pornography:[6]

1. Ninety-three percent of boys and sixty-two percent of girls are exposed to Internet pornography before the age of eighteen.

2. Seventy percent of boys have spent more than thirty consecutive minutes looking at online porn on at least one occasion.

3. Twenty-three percent of girls have spent more than thirty consecutive minutes looking at online porn on at least one occasion; fourteen percent have done it on more than one occasion.

4. Eighty-three percent of boys and fifty-seven percent of girls have seen group sex on the Internet.

5. Sixty-nine percent of boys and fifty-five percent of girls have seen porn showing same-sex intercourse.

6. Thirty-nine percent of boys and twenty-three percent of girls have seen online sex acts involving bondage.

7. Thirty-two percent of boys and eighteen percent of girls have viewed bestiality on the Internet.

8. Eighteen percent of boys and ten percent of girls have seen rape or sexual violence online.

9. Fifteen percent of boys and nine percent of girls have seen child pornography.

10. Only three percent of boys and seventeen percent of girls have never seen online pornography.

Take a moment to reflect on the sobering reality of these numbers. Witnessing group sex online is normative for adolescents. Seeing same-sex intercourse is now a "typical" developmental experience as well. One in three children is exposed to bondage or domination-themed sexual acts. Clearly the types of sex that our children are exposed to are changing.

Stewarding our children's sexuality means we must equip ourselves with the information, insights, and engagement necessary to offset the influence of these messages. We must talk honestly and directly about these images that young people are seeing, because they are shaping and distorting their reality. If we do not begin this difficult conversation with them, we will lose a generation of the church. As Josh McDowell states, we're just one click away.[7]

While proponents of promiscuous sexual lifestyles and pro-pornography groups would lead you to believe that viewing this content has no impact on the developing mind, the science suggests otherwise. A review of previous studies conducted by Mike Allen and peers suggests that aggression levels increase in boys who view online pornography.[8] Also, Chiara Sabina and colleagues found that both boys and girls experience disgust (fifty-one percent of girls, twenty percent of boys), shock (seventy-eight percent of girls, sixty-five percent of boys), and shame (thirty-two percent of both boys and girls) following exposure to pornographic material, while nearly twenty percent felt unattractive or inadequate about themselves after seeing porn.[9] Pornography is not some harmless leisure pursuit; it shapes the very essence of self in those who consume it. What we watch matters—especially when we are young.

It is difficult for parents to come to terms with the fact that children develop into sexual beings. Parents often delay important conversations about sexuality, frequently out of the desire to maintain children's innocence. Given these statistics, it is necessary to have an open conversation with children about what they have already been exposed to. When developmental processes that are already happening are not discussed, children are suffering in silence.

In discussing pornography and any other area of sexual content your children might have been exposed to, open-ended questions are the most helpful. They enable you to gather as much information as possible in a nonthreatening manner. Questions beginning with "What" are more useful than questions starting with "Why." Here are some examples for you to consider, keeping in mind that these questions cover a wide range and that the questions you ask must be age-appropriate for the child.[10]

1. Have you ever seen pictures or movies of naked people/ pornography online? If so, how did you find them? Who showed you or told you about these pictures or movies?

2. What was happening in the images? How long did you look at them?

3. When you first saw the images, what did you begin to feel inside? Did you feel embarrassed or guilty about looking at the images? What was happening in your body?

4. What were your thoughts about their naked bodies? Did you notice anything different about their bodies compared to your own body?

Again, the age of the child will determine the type of questions you will ask and the level of detail you can expect in his or her response. Some parents turn a blind eye, believing it's just part of growing up. Others prefer to converse with their child about the images at a later date and time. The topic should be addressed as soon as it is discovered, especially if you find your child viewing them.

Unfortunately, most parents do not have a plan for how they will deal with this situation. None of us want our children to think we are afraid to talk about it or that we don't care enough to educate them or that we are giving them permission to continue viewing it. Our silence betrays us if we do not speak truth in those awkward but important moments. The first occurrence should set into motion this conversation, including a set of boundaries for proper Internet use and agreed-upon consequences for failure to maintain the agreement. This is an example of how a product such as Covenant Eyes can be extremely helpful in developing accountability with your kids.

From a spiritual standpoint, this dabbling in pornography becomes an open door to talk to our kids about the incredible beauty of the human body. Rather than condemning their curiosity and shaming them—creating a "forbidden fruit syndrome" that results in their continued desire for something they cannot have, which causes them to hide their behavior a la Adam and Eve in Genesis 3—we can remind our children that we are "fearfully and wonderfully made" (Psalm 139:14), that our bodies are not our own but "temples of the Holy Spirit" (1 Corinthians 6:19-20), and that the primary function of human sexuality is to deepen the emotional and spiritual intimacy within the marriage covenant (Mark 10:8).

"Sexting"

The glow of her screen stood out against the darkness of her bedroom. "Send me a pic" the text read. Her heart pounded as she snapped a picture. With trembling hands, she typed his name and hit "Send." In the darkness, she gave her thirteen-year-old innocence away to a boy who cared nothing about her.

This story is not an uncommon one. As demonstrated by the suicides of eighteen-year-old Jesse Logan in Ohio in 2008 and thirteen-year-old Hope Witsell in Florida in 2009, the consequences are devastating when sexts go viral within a community.

Through these stories and others like them, it is clear that "sexting" has become another technology-driven trend that we *must* talk about with our children. "Sexting" can be defined as the sending of nude or sexual photos and videos through a cellular or electronic medium, such as a tablet or cell phone. *The Social Costs of Pornography* cites that in 2009, twenty-two percent of adolescent females ages thirteen to nineteen and thirty-six percent of young women ages twenty to twenty-six had sent nude photos or videos of themselves.[11] More recently, the

National Campaign released statistics suggesting that twenty percent of teens overall have sent "sexts," and forty-eight percent have received such images.[12] It is safe to assume that the actual numbers are even higher. British teenagers in one focus group described "sexting" and hardcore pornography as so common in their world that it was considered "mundane."[13] As with other sexual exploits, we can assume that shame keeps more accurate numbers from being disclosed. What most parents and kids forget is that distributors and recipients of "sexts" are participating in a felony, as three boys from West Springfield High School in Northern Virginia discovered the hard way.[14]

According to sexual addiction expert and licensed clinical social worker Rob Weiss, smartphone apps have become similar to crack cocaine for the tech generation.[15] They are cheap, easy to use, and offer an ever-changing supply of sexual partners. "Sexting" is thought to be safe among adolescents and teenagers due to smartphone apps such as Sizzle, Twitter, Facebook Poke, and the biggest culprit, Snapchat, which deletes photos automatically one to ten seconds after the recipient opens them. These apps create the belief in the user that there are no consequences for sending pictures as they cannot be saved or distributed in any way. If we have learned anything with the advent of technology, we have learned this: once an item is sent, it is always saved *somewhere.*

The biggest benefit we can provide to our children is to talk to them about the realities of the virtual landscape and equip them with information about what to do when exposed to the sexually explicit materials they will encounter there. In starting "the conversation" when they are young, we can equip them with tools that will serve them in a variety of contexts involving sexual decision-making.

The following tips for parents who want to protect their kids from "sexting" are adapted from <internetsafety101.org>.[16]

1. Talk to your kids about what they are doing online, and start when they are young. Outline the risks for them, and start them off with online activities that you can do together.

2. Make sure your kids know that once a message is sent over the phone or the Internet, it is not private and it is not anonymous. It can be—and likely will be—forwarded to others. Be sure to keep track of what your kids are posting online.

3. Know who your kids are connecting with online. When they are younger, you can instill healthy habits by creating shared accounts to use together.

4. Place limits on the use of electronic devices. The more they use these devices, the more likely they are to stumble into inappropriate territory. Model balance for them, and hold them to a reasonable amount of time on their devices.

5. Set expectations about the use of electronic devices, and follow through on consequences for the inappropriate use of these devices.

6. Ask questions regularly. "Have you ever sent or received a nude image? Have you ever been pressured to send one? What could happen if you did send one? Who would you tell if you received one?"

Much like pornography, "sexting" is the gross objectification of the human form. While pornography is very much laden with fantasy, sexting has a much more personal quality about it. Viewers don't know the porn stars in the videos; they do know the neighbors, classmates, and friends they see in "sexts." Sadly, the sender and the receiver perceive the body as an object rather than experiencing the soul of the person who dwells within that body. There is no understanding of the essence of humanity embodied in the other, only a desire to take gratification at the expense of the other.

Sex has become a significant idol in American culture, and "sexting" is a driving force in creating this reality in generation "sext." With this in mind, we must fully live the words from 1 John 5:21—"Dear children, keep yourselves from idols." There are a variety of software products that can help you steward your children's sexuality by actively monitoring their technology use.

Masturbation

While sexual intercourse has long been perceived as a coming-of-age experience in American culture, masturbation is the exploratory process that sets the wheels of the sexual appetite in motion. As the old adage suggests, ninety-nine percent of men do it and the other one percent lie about it. This statement could probably be added to our list of myths about male sexuality from chapter three, but it may not be far off base. Regardless, the social pressure on teens and young adults is staggering. In the 2010 National Survey of Sexual Health and Behavior, researchers reported that sixty-two percent of fourteen- to fifteen-year-old males and forty percent of females had masturbated. Among sixteen- to seventeen-year-olds the percentage had risen to seventy-five percent of boys and forty-five percent of young women. By eighteen or nineteen, the results indicate that eighty-one percent of males and sixty percent of females masturbate.[17] Given the freedom with which masturbation is talked about in our culture, you will need to be intentional about facilitating this conversation about masturbation with your children—both boys *and* girls. It is not just a male issue anymore. You need to identify your sexual value system and where masturbation fits in. Most Christian parents I talk with fit into one of two broad categories: abstinence and moderation.

Abstinence implies exactly that: abstaining from the practice. The goal voiced by many parents who self-identify in this category is the growth of virtues of purity, self-control, and patience, as well as delaying the gratification of orgasm until the wedding night. Among parents who are more inclined to approach masturbation from the perspective of moderation, there are certain guidelines to implement. Among these guidelines are *frequency*—not engaging in the behavior regularly; *fantasy*—not using mental images to stimulate arousal; *functionality*—not using masturbation to feel better or change moods; *fidelity*—being honest and trustworthy when asked about the practice; and *faith*—plugging into accountability with a youth pastor or a mentor in the church to keep the practice from becoming problematic. Whichever approach you find yourself identifying with more, be sure that you are able to communicate your beliefs to your kids in language they can understand.

Masturbation begins as sexual exploration and may be later used more problematically to experience pleasure, escape, or release. The rise in sexual behaviors involving bondage-domination-sadism-masochism among adolescents and teens adds a disturbing twist. The practice of limiting oxygen flow to the brain to enhance the experience of orgasm can lead to autoerotic asphyxiation—accidental death by strangulation during masturbation. Below are five key questions or observations to keep in mind regarding autoerotic asphyxiation.

"Need to Know" Information about Choking Behaviors[18]

1. Have you seen bruises on the neck or shoulders of a child or adolescent that might be indicative of choking games?

2. Do you notice or hear complaints of unusual or unexplained genital pain or injuries in your child or adolescent?

3. Does your child or adolescent express concerns about sexual matters, even vaguely?

4. Do you notice a pattern of bruising on the wrists, ankles, arms, legs, and torso that might suggest binding or bond-

age-related activities? Have genitalia or other body parts been pierced?

5. Have you heard talk about or witnessed choking games or other risky behavior involving oxygen loss or fainting in your child or adolescent or his or her friends?

Oral Sex

Because oral sex has been deemed *not* sex in large measure in secular culture, its rise to prominence in American relationships has been meteoric. The previously cited sexual survey demonstrates a similar trend in increasing oral sex among teenagers. Male teenagers are more likely to report that oral sex benefits the relationship with their partner, whereas females report feeling used, guilty, or hurt by the experience. The previously cited sexual survey demonstrates a similar trend in increasing oral sex among teenagers with twelve percent, thirty-one percent, and fifty-four percent of males reporting receiving oral sex from a female at the ages of fourteen to fifteen, sixteen to seventeen, and eighteen to nineteen years of age respectively.[19] When surveyed, a group of ninth graders reported the top five reasons they engage in oral sex: (5) it's less risky than vaginal sex, (4) curiosity, (3) gaining popularity, (2) improving relationships, and (1) seeking pleasure.[20] In spite of the belief that it is safer than vaginal sex, oral sex has been linked to throat cancer as well as the spread of disease. The simple truth is this: oral sex is not abstinence—it is sex with the mouth.

Think back to the chapter on male and female sexual myths. Oral sex among teenagers and in pornography exists at the epitome of this collective mythology. The lack of face-to-face connection during oral sex embodies objectification. The posture of the male receiving oral sex is one of power, looking down on his object of pleasure, and the intensity of pleasure is largely experienced alone in oral sex. Tragically, teenage girls and young women who engage in providing oral sex believe that their experience of love, acceptance, beauty, and significance is bound up in performing this act.

Our children are created to be known and understood and to participate in the fullness of community within the family. When our lives become too busy for them, they seek out affirmation and validation where they can get it: their peers. In chapter six we will explore the importance of the attachment process and what you can do to connect with your kids. As your sons or daughters grow into later childhood and the teenage years, your conversations with them about their sexuality must include discussions on oral sex.

Video Chatting

Another tool that has been used by teenagers and children to explore their sexuality is the webcam. Video chatting via products such as Skype, iChat, Google Talk, and FaceTime makes the world a much smaller place and enables connection with people who live across the country or across the globe. My children use video chatting as a way to stay connected to grandparents and other family members who live hundreds of miles away. It gives all parties involved the opportunity to connect face to face and catch up on what is happening in life.

According to a study done by the Pew Research Center in 2012, forty percent of teens report video chatting with friends, either one-on-one or in a chat room.[21] This familiarity with technology is leaving children prone to online predation and bullying with peers. According to <internetsafety101.org>, the majority of Internet-based sex crimes are initiated in chat rooms. Additionally, one in seven kids will receive a sexual solicitation online, with fifty-six percent being asked to send a picture and twenty-seven percent of those requests being sexual in nature. Sexual solicitations of children are most likely to occur in a chat room, instant message program, or other programs such as social media or gaming sites. Be sure to talk with your children about the dangers of online predators as they begin to use chatting features to connect with their social world.[22]

Facebook, YouTube, and Social Media Sites

It makes sense that if kids are using webcams to connect, they will eventually use webcams to capture videos of themselves. The culprit for many of the bizarre adolescent and teenager-produced videos can be found on Facebook, YouTube, and other sites. While not necessarily pornographic in nature in and of itself, YouTube is brimming with adult content that is inappropriate for children. Many parents are unaware of the Children's Online Privacy Protection Act, which is a law mandating that children be thirteen before using any social media accounts.[23]

As was stated previously, even children not looking for pornography may stumble upon it in three clicks or less. Like many web sites with adult content, access to the content on YouTube is quite easy to get to. Only three percent of pornographic web sites require proof of age before granting access to sexually explicit material. And while YouTube does require an account to be created that verifies age, most children can do the math and crack the code to gain admission. Making this process even more problematic is that approximately seventy-five percent of pornographic web sites display visual teasers on their homepages prior to asking if viewers are aware of legal age. Before your child may recognize it, he or she is sucked into a sexual vortex on the Internet from which escape can be difficult.[24]

With all the visually based stimulation available in our children's world, it is important to have conversations with them about their eyes and what they see. You may want them to forget what they have seen, but their brains will not, especially if it was simultaneously fascinating and strangely pleasing, as most sexual content tends to be. Psalm 101:3 states, "I will not look with approval on anything that is vile." In Matthew 6:22-23, Christ addresses stewarding our children's sexuality by protecting their eyes:

The eye is the lamp of the body. If your eyes are healthy, your whole body will be full of light. But if your eyes are unhealthy, your whole body will be full of darkness. If then the light within you is darkness, how great is that darkness!

Homosexuality

Another unavoidable trend in American culture is homosexuality. Depicted regularly on prime-time television, it is not a conversation that can be avoided in raising sexually healthy children. Within Christianity are a number of diverse perspectives on how to understand homosexuality. We must communicate our values clearly. While it is important to operate from a biblical basis in teaching our children about sexuality, it is also important that they see modeled the compassion of Christ demonstrated in John 8.

We do not know the details of the transgression committed by the woman who was brought before Jesus to be stoned, only that it involved adultery. The details of her story are a moot point; the detail we need to pay attention to is Christ's response. His words suggest that he will not condemn her *and* that she go and leave her life of sin. In the church we are called to focus on equipping others to live free from the influence of sin; condemnation will be taken care of accordingly. As Dan Boone states, "Perhaps we should leave the wielding of the sword to Christ. Let's allow him to be the one who overturns the tables and drives the money-changers from his house."[25]

Sexual Abuse

Other than losing a child to death, the thing parents fear most is that their children will experience sexual abuse. The Centers for Disease Control and Prevention suggests that one in six boys and one in four girls will be abused before the age of eighteen.[26]

With scandals in the church, abuse in the schools, and graphic descriptions of perpetration on the nightly news, we live acutely aware of the sexual trauma that many children in our culture are subjected to. It occurs equally across urban and rural areas, across race, culture, and socioeconomic status. Childhood sexual abuse can involve a variety of behaviors that include kissing, fondling, genital contact, showing pornography, exposure of genitalia, voyeurism or ogling, and verbal pressure for sex. Most abuse occurs at the hands of someone the child knows and trusts, including family members and acquaintances such as a babysitter, neighbor, childcare provider, or family friend. Boys are more likely to be abused by someone outside of the family, while girls are more likely to experience sexual abuse at the hands of someone they know. Only ten percent of sexual abuse occurs with a stranger.[27]

Signs a child has been victimized include angry outbursts, an increase in nightmares or other sleep-related disturbances, anxiety, depression, difficulty walking or sitting, withdrawal or social isolation, and an increase in sexual interest or use of sexual language.[28] If you suspect abuse, encourage the child to talk about his or her experiences, and reassure the child that he or she did nothing wrong. Be careful not to coerce information or lead in any way. If the child confirms abuse, or if your instincts tell you something is off in the child's denial, seek psychological help and a medical evaluation as needed.

Parental Advisory

Discussing this sexual content, along with whatever trend comes next, is an essential job for all parents. While talking with children is a necessary part of this responsibility, other steps are appropriate as well. If you have a child who has access to an Internet-connectable device such as an iPad, Kindle, or iPod Touch, there are a few safety strategies you can implement, according to Scott McClurg of Covenant Eyes.[29]

First, be aware of the apps that your children are downloading. By sharing a log-in for their accounts, you can always be in the know about what apps are being loaded. As a general rule of thumb, if you're paying for the device or the use of the device, you should be setting ground rules about the *use* of the device. In addition to knowing what apps are being downloaded to your child's device, also know that certain apps allow for backdoor Internet access or for social contact between users. Example categories include social media apps and some games. Know what your child is asking about by doing your research; a game or app may look innocent on the surface but may contain more than it appears to at first glance. Also, be sure to do app inventories, especially with younger children.

If you share a log-in, chances are that the apps you download will also show up on their devices. Purchasing tablets created specifically for the use of children, such as a Nabi, is a step in the right direction.

Last, know how to lock down the devices that your children are being trusted with. Part of teaching our children good stewardship of their electronic resources is modeling for them how to manage devices and providing boundaries that keep them safe as they use them. You can find video tutorials and other helpful resources at <covenanteyes.com> for how to lock down your iOS and Android-based devices.

Generation "sext" is a cohort of young adults, teens, and children who have been born into a world of instant accessibility and immediate gratification. The world is literally at their fingertips. They have been shaped and defined by the technology that they use to connect with their world, and with that they have been exposed to the thrill and pleasure of sexuality in a variety of developmentally inappropriate ways.

Our challenge is twofold: to *protect* our children from the influence of sexualized culture by *educating* them about sex, their bodies, and God's design for human sexuality. This task of stewarding our children's sexuality is reflected in Proverbs 22:6—"Start children off on the way they should go, and even when they are old they will not turn from it."

six

POWER SURGE
SEX AND DEVELOPMENT

Kapow! For the parents of adolescents, life changes in an instant. One day your son and the girl next door are playmates, and the next he's acting goofy, tripping over his suddenly clumsy feet, and trying to act tough in front of his friends. Middle schools and church youth groups are the petri dishes in which life's hormonal experiments take place. Nature lights the fuse of puberty, and the rest of us are left ducking for cover. The good news is that you survived it years ago, and you now have a puberty survival guide here at your disposal.

Other similar explosions will occur during pubescence when your children will have to navigate the suddenly sexual world they have become aware of. It is the biological clock that all young adults have ticking inside them. Fantasy, pornography, and experimentation are all discovered as the body changes. As your children grow older, they will be influenced less by you and more by their peers. Therefore, your monitoring of behavior will bring about more frequent and intense discussion.

Of course, each child will be different in how he or she responds to his or her biological time clock, and you will need to be flexible, firm, and consistent. However, do not back down from the values you are helping instill in your children.

Healthy parenting involves explaining the biological processes of puberty to children. If knowledge is power, it is better we empower our kids to make healthy choices rather than letting them be shaped by the influence of peers and culture. Author Larry Daly outlines seven suggestions to discuss puberty and the biological changes that will occur in your children: [1]

1. Inform children at an early age that somewhere between ages eight and thirteen positive biological changes will be happening in their bodies.

2. As they get closer to puberty, discuss the changes that will occur in their bodies, such as the growth of pubic hair, the changing of the voice, and growth of breasts (in young women).

3. Discuss with daughters what happens when they have their first period. This will be specifically addressed in the following section on menarche and menstruation.

4. Identify what happens to the body, such as clothes not fitting, getting taller, putting on muscle, enjoying foods they once disliked, attraction to the opposite sex, menarche in females, and nocturnal emission in males.

5. Talk openly with your children about what happens the first day they shower with other boys or girls and how other children's bodies will appear different from their own. Inform them that discomfort might be normal but that they have nothing to be ashamed of.

6. Discuss also what may not be happening. They may notice that everyone else around them is changing biologically but nothing is happening to them. It is not uncommon

that some children do not reach puberty until later in their teen years, which can lead to depression, anxiety, and self-esteem concerns in children who see that they're not developing at the same rate as their friends.

7. Last, talk about why puberty occurs and how God made the human body to go through specific biological steps in preparation for adulthood.

These seven suggestions are designed to assist you in discussing the evolution of your child's body and provide you with opportunities to sit down and talk to your child about sex. Because children enter into puberty at different times, the decision needs to be based upon your observations of the development of your child's body. It is up to you to begin to discuss the significance of sex. It may take years for children to completely understand the details and issues surrounding sex and their changing bodies. Be patient. Take time to sit down and explain what is happening to them and what these changes actually mean. The START model introduced in chapter eight will help guide you through this process.

Menarche and Menstruation

When it comes to raising daughters, having a firm understanding of the menstrual process is essential. Laurie Heap, a Kansas City-based OB/GYN and natural hormone replacement specialist, has worked extensively with women of all ages in this area. She has developed the acronym "WOMAN" to help you remember these important aspects of helping your daughter understand and steward her changing body.

When a girl has her first period, which is called menarche in medical terms, it can be a distressing time—for everyone in the family. The hormonal changes going on in her body can create mood swings, irritability, headaches, and other symptoms that make it difficult to handle and can also be a challenge to facilitating meaningful conversations. Keeping the lines of communication open with your daughter during this time of change in her life is important, but it can feel like a minefield. The following simple facts and strategies can help you and your daughter make this era of life a positive experience for your relationship.

W: What Is Normal?

In the first year after a girl starts having periods, it is normal to have some irregularity and for her emotions to be a bit unpredictable. Simply knowing this puts many moms and daughters at ease. A woman's cycle is not just having a period. The menstrual cycle refers to the first day of her period to the last day before the first day of her next period. This time frame can vary from month to month. Only fifteen percent of women have a twenty-eight-day cycle, and the normal range is between twenty-four and thirty-eight days.[2]

The hormone changes that occur at menarche are dramatic. Estrogen and progesterone are the two major hormones of the menstrual cycle. Estrogen, which is low until menarche, begins to rise in the first half of a woman's cycle and signals the brain to release a hormone called luteinizing hormone (LH). This surge of LH from the brain causes the ovaries to ovulate and release an egg. After ovulation, estrogen levels decrease, and progesterone rises and then falls. The decrease in progesterone leads to a woman's period, and the whole process starts over again. It is normal for the first part of a woman's cycle—from the first day of the period to ovulation—to vary from one cycle to the next in response to physical and psychological stress or illness. It is not normal for the time from ovulation to the beginning of the next cycle to vary by more than three days from one cycle to the next. If the hormones are rising and falling in this balance, women should have a sense of well-being, youth, and vitality. Dramatic mood swings, painful periods, headaches, cyclical depression, and severe acne are all signs of hormone imbalance.[3]

It is important for young women to understand what estrogen and progesterone do in other systems of their bodies. These sex hormones do not just run the reproductive system. The balance between estrogen and progesterone that occurs during the menstrual cycle over approximately thirty days has positive and negative effects that perfectly balance each other in the brain, the bones, the breasts, and the cardiovascular system, just to name a few. There are estrogen and progesterone receptors all over a woman's body. They affect the—

Cardiovascular system: Estrogen increases blood pressure; progesterone lowers it. Estrogen decreases insulin resistance; progesterone increases it. Estrogen increases the ability of the blood to clot; progesterone normalizes it. Estrogen lowers cholesterol; progesterone increases it.[4]

Brain: Estrogen levels throughout the reproductive years have a protective effect for Alzheimer's disease. Estrogen wakes up the brain; progesterone calms it and has an antidepressant and antianxiety effect on the chemicals in the brain. Premenstrual syndrome is associated with low progesterone after ovulation. The balance between estrogen and progesterone affects how the brains of women develop, and a woman's brain is not fully developed until age twenty-four.[5] Natural hormone balance is important in these last ten years of brain development and is responsible for giving women the wonderful qualities we love about them: untiring generosity, the ability to multitask, interpersonal detailed orientation, deep spirituality, and a gentle strength. Hormones wire a woman's brain to provide these qualities to take care of loved ones throughout her life!

Breasts: Estrogen has a detrimental effect in the breast. It has been shown to cause DNA damage that leads to a breast cancer cell formation, and it causes breast cells to divide more rapidly. Progesterone, however, protects breast cells from the damage caused by estrogen and slows cell division.[6]

Bone: Estrogen builds bone, while progesterone breaks down bone. This type of balance between building up and breaking down is necessary to increase bone density throughout the teen years and the twenties.[7]

There are many other effects of these two amazing hormones seen in the skin, the immune system, fat cells, and digestion—to name a few. Young women need to know that their cycle affects much more in their bodies than just reproduction; living in a state of natural hormone balance is about promoting the health of their entire bodies. Synthetic hormones from a variety of sources disrupt this balance and have negative effects throughout the body. Having a conversation with your daughter about these issues and talking with her gynecologist about the impact of synthetic hormones on her health are important.

O: Observations

Observations help your daughter learn to track her cycle. Teaching your daughter to chart her cycle and observe the changes that occur helps her understand her body and makes the hormonal changes less frightening. Charting the cycle gives her a sense of influence over the changes occurring in her body. It also helps you communicate with her about these changes and what she is feeling. If you are interested in charting, you can visit <http://nfp.marquette.edu>. Read through the instructions with your daughter, and print off a chart for your personal use. You can also attend a class together on charting. To find a class, visit the FertilityCare Centers of America and search in your area. There are also apps such as <nfṗchartingonline.com>.

M: Managing Symptoms and Emotions

Charting helps you communicate and track the symptoms and emotional changes you or your daughters are trying to manage. Your daughter can anticipate the week when she may need a little more time for herself or a little more coaching from you. This biological transformation can be overwhelming. Building in breaks for exercise and relaxation based on where she is in her cycle can help, especially in the first year of her cycle.

A: Attaching Sex to a Sacramental Purpose

Charting also attaches sex to a higher purpose, namely connecting spiritually with one's spouse. In the time leading up to ovulation, the cervix produces a fluid that results in the fertile window during a woman's cycle. Recognizing the potential for bringing new life into the world and recording that on her chart help connect this time of change to the likelihood of conception. The ability to bring a new soul into existence is not something to be taken lightly, and having a period is just one part of this wonderful gift.

N: Natural Hormone Balance

Balance is the key to treatment of women's hormone-related problems. Premenstrual syndrome, irregular cycles after the first year, painful periods not relieved by a little ibuprofen, and hormone-related acne are all signs of hormone imbalance—and are not things your daughter may just have to live with. If your daughter is charting, she will have a very good idea of how her symptoms correspond to where she is in her cycle. You can also talk to her about signs of hormone imbalance, such as brown bleeding of three or more days at the tail end of her period, three or more days of spotting leading up to her period, a very small amount of cervical fluid (normal amount is around four to seven days), variability of the last half of her cycle by three or more days from one month to the next, or periods that are too light or too heavy.[8] All these are signs that something is out of balance hormonally. Charting helps her see physical signs or symptoms that are often nonspecific and frustrating. The solution is to implement dietary and lifestyle changes, certain vitamin supplements for specific symptoms, and if all these fail, to seek out a physician who will help restore balance to her body without using synthetic hormones and other medications that mask symptoms while failing to correct the underlying problem.

Understanding and Communicating the Spiritual Aspects of Sex

While it is important to understand and communicate the body's physical changes and biological aspects of sex, it is equally important to address the spiritual aspects of sex. Much of the historical criticism of the field of sexology centers on reductionism, or seeing the physical act of sex as a fundamentally physical act rather than an act involving the whole person—spiritual and emotional. Scientifically, sex has been defined as an overtly biological act involving the body. Within the church, this ideology has been further perpetuated by *dualism*, or the belief that the physical body and spiritual aspects of the self are inherently separate and do not influence one another. We believe that the body is "bad" and the spirit is "good." While the spirit we have been created with is certainly good as it is a reflection of God himself (Genesis 1:26), we need to explore Paul's writings before we lump the body into the exclusively "bad" category. Paul refers to the flesh and the body in his writings.

Mark Hayse, professor of Christian education at MidAmerica Nazarene University in Olathe, Kansas, suggests that the *flesh* be more properly understood as a sin principle, a representation of rebellion and selfishness, while the *body* pertains to our wonderfully created human physiology, as well as a metaphor for the church.[9] It is with this basic principle in mind that we can begin to understand the fullness of our sexual design.

Two becoming "one flesh" is more than a scriptural euphemism for intercourse (Genesis 2:24; Mark 10:8). It is a depiction of surrendering our personal desires to create a bond that is greater than the sum of its parts. We prize our spouse; we cherish our spouse. Yet when we live in a dualistic mind-set in our Christian marriages, we run the risk of reducing our spouse to body parts and pieces. Raising sexually healthy children begins with a healthy expression of intimacy. Praying together, holding hands in the car, and complimenting one another lay the foundation for healthy intimacy, sexual and otherwise, and models for our children that we are more than just physical beings.

Because of the vulnerability involved in intercourse, it *must* be approached from a place of emotional balance and spiritual connection. Talking together, laughing together, touching non-sexually, worshiping together, praying together, and eating dinner together—they all matter.

All too often we see sex viewed as the only tool for creating intimacy in marriage. "How's that workin' for ya?" Dr. Phil would ask. Truth is, it probably isn't. Sex is designed to be the *fulfillment* of intimacy, not the *totality* of intimacy. Just because a teenager's body is ready for sex doesn't mean that the teenager is. This is a message our kids are desperate to hear.

We must be faithful to equip our children to make healthy sexual choices in the tsunami of sexuality that exists in American culture. As Paul writes in 1 Corinthians 4:1-2,

This, then, is how you ought to regard us: as servants of Christ and as those entrusted with the mysteries God has revealed. Now it is required that those who have been given a trust must prove faithful.

seven

NESTER OR NOMAD
SEX AND ATTACHMENT

When you think about what people tend to desire in life, it's easy to consider items such as a bigger television, a better job, or a relaxing home on the beach. Our culture tells us these are the things we are designed for. While our experiences and personalities do shape our preferences, we are created to be understood as more than a salary figure, the size of our television screen, or the zip code of our home.

Another object of desire in our culture is certain foods. What is the number-one treat you crave? Perhaps it is a certain candy bar, a favorite dessert, or a mouth-watering entrée at a local restaurant. Though we each have our cravings, we are created to crave something more—something deeper. This need is *connec-*

tion. Todd Frye, chair of the Counselor Education Department at MidAmerica Nazarene University, expounds on connection in the following section.[1]

Connection is sometimes overlooked as one of our greatest human needs, because we often lack perspective. We tend to look toward those things that bring us immediate gratification rather than those enduring needs that are crucial to our long-term existence.

When the spark of relationship is not instant, we move on in search of quick and easy means of getting our needs met. This McDonald's mentality in our culture hampers our ability to know and be known in relationship. As parents, spouses, and friends, we need to embody a reflective perspective that exposes our deep need for connection with other human beings. From the cry of a newborn baby to the goodbye at the end of the earthly journey, the need for connection defines our human existence from the cradle to the grave.

This longing for connection is known in psychological terms as *attachment.* Attachment is a proximity maintenance system that is hardwired within all of us to monitor and protect us from feeling too distant from those we consider to be our primary forms of connection.[2] The individuals that represent our closest connections are considered primary attachment figures. Parents and spouses typically fill that role in our lives, while some individuals develop secondary attachment figures such as a grandparent, sibling, teacher, or coach. However, these secondary attachment figures cannot replace all the functions of the primary attachment system found in parent-child and spousal relationships.

The primary function of the attachment system is to ensure that certain physical and emotional needs are being met. These needs are essential to our sense of survival through life. Though many of these needs can be artificially taken care of on our own, they are most fully experienced in the context of relationship.

These primary attachment needs are *comfort, protection, acceptance,* and *overall safety.*[3] From the moment we are born we are dependent on our attachment figures to meet these needs. Infants who pass away due to a lack of physical touch—a phenomenon known as "failure to thrive"—provide evidence for this truth.

Another example is the "stranger danger" that children experience in certain situations. When someone the child doesn't know well enough to feel safe enters the child's space, the reflex is to seek out our attachment figures for protection. A child in this situation might hold onto or hide behind his or her parent's legs in hopes the parent will give protection from this potential threat. When the frightened child is picked up and reassured and feels protected, he or she begins to believe the parent will be there when needed. These moment-by-moment interactions with the primary attachment figure build a framework for how the child views himself or herself and the world. Parents must maintain a certain posture with the child to ensure that the child's attachment needs are met. According to Frye, this posture can be represented in the acronym "CARE."[4]

C for Curious: In order for children to feel accepted and wanted, they need to experience their parents being curious about them. The basic question the child has for the parent is "Am I lovable enough for you to be curious about me?" Parental curiosity is exhibited toward children through interactions such as "Tell me more about your pretty drawing" or "How do you feel when you can't play the same video games as your friends?" This curiosity communicates that the parent is interested in the child's internal world. It suggests to the child that his or her experiences are important and that the parent is interested in knowing him or her. The experience of being known in the mind of another offers a sense of security for the child, to realize that he or she is not alone in the world.[5]

A for Accessible:[6] Accessibility answers the child's question "Will you be there for me when I need you?" Parents who operate as secure attachment figures are perceived as being reachable by their children. These parents make themselves available physically and emotionally, and when they are around their children, they are flexible enough to stop what they are doing to hear their children. "In a minute" shuts down the connection children are seeking. Most parents need to work a little harder at being accessible to their children.

Two of the greatest threats to accessibility are parental busyness and preoccupation. In a world that demands so much efficiency to complete tasks, we often value efficiency over accessibility. Busyness and preoccupation communicate to our children that we are not attuned to their needs and not easily reachable. Technology such as smartphones, tablets, and laptops make us eternally accessible to the demands of work, often at the expense of accessibility to our children. They know that we are more attuned to our phones than to them. From the children's perspective, the lack of accessibility is threatening, because they cannot get our attention if they feel scared, hurt, or any other variety of emotions or experiences that need an attachment response. When we are inaccessible, our children feel alone in the world. Like Christ on the cross, they wonder if they have been deserted.

R for Responsive:[7] Responsive parents perceive and address their children's attachment requests. Responsiveness answers the question "Will you come when I call you?" Some parents make themselves accessible physically but are still not responsive. Nightmares are a great example of this dynamic. A terrified child who is screaming for Mommy or Daddy in the dead of night is in tremendous need of responsive parenting. The child needs to be calmed and soothed and be made to feel secure. Staying in our own bed because we believe the child needs to learn to deal with his or her fears creates a powerful wound in the parent-child relationship and may result in the child's first relational trauma. The child begins to believe that the parents are unwilling or unable to meet his or her attachment needs.

If this occurs repeatedly, over time inappropriate self-soothing begins as the child learns to meet his or her own needs in isolation versus having those needs met in relationship. As these children become adults, this self-soothing transforms into sexual addiction, gambling, disordered eating, and a host of other struggles. Many parents are afraid of being *too* responsive to their children for fear of developing an unhealthy dependence. On the contrary, parents who are attuned and responsive tend to raise children who exhibit healthy dependence and a strong sense of self.

E for Engaged:[8] There's a difference between being responsive and being engaged. The primary question in the area of engagement is "Will my parent stay with me long enough and well enough until I return to calmness and connection?" Some parents who are responsive don't stay engaged long enough to bring their child back to the level of comfort he or she needs. The parent meets the physical needs of the child without considering the child's emotional needs. Using the stranger danger example, the disengaged parent might pick up the child but be inclined to put him or her down again before the emotional experience of fear has been defused. Soothing tones, gentle eye contact, and relaxed facial expressions are the key ingredients of healthy responsiveness and engagement. An engaged response completes the circle of CARE that ensures the child that his or her attachment figure is there and will continue to be there as a secure base and safe haven. The child begins to explore his or her world confidently, knowing that he or she is loved.

Safe and Secure

You probably played tag when you were a child. This recess pastime is an essential developmental experience. A child doesn't have to be the fastest kid on the playground as long as he or she knows one critical piece of information: the location of home base.

When we got a new puppy at our house, my boys created a home base for themselves on the landing where Duke would not be able to nibble their toes or bite their pants. This home base is similar to how children use their parents as a secure base in life.

The home base serves as a safe haven during the times when life threatens attachment needs. The experiences of being scared, feeling ashamed, hurting physically or emotionally, or exhibiting sadness prime the child's return to home base to find value and safety.

Think back to when your children were just learning to walk. They waddled away for a few moments, examined the world around them, and then toddled back to you to check in and make sure you hadn't gone anywhere. When home base is secure and consistent, it gives children the freedom to leave the base and engage the world with confidence, creativity, and self-assurance. This is important to children's development as they learn to explore and learn about life away from the home base. As they grow, they are able to carry this notion of a home base with them, even when the parents are not physically present. Secure attachment is truly the foundation of faith.

If children do not experience CARE, they will question the security of the base and will tend to hover around the attachment figure out of fear. If the CARE is inconsistent, they begin to take on disorganized qualities or will search out another home base where their attachment needs are met.[9] To paraphrase Dorothy, "There's no place like home [base]!"

According to Curt Thompson, author of *Anatomy of the Soul*, children who utilize their parents as a secure base "develop emotional elasticity in the face of stress, build healthy relationships with peers, and establish a sense of emotional equilibrium within their own minds."[10]

Free to Attach: Attachment Styles

Research on attachment began in the 1960s and 1970s with John Bowlby and his colleague, Mary Ainsworth. Through their research, Bowlby and Ainsworth identified four attachment styles: *secure attachment, anxious attachment, avoidant attachment,* and *fearful attachment.*[11]

These styles tend to be stable throughout life—even into adulthood—unless they are challenged by alternative emotional experiences in adult attachment relationships, most notably the marriage relationship. These four patterns demonstrate the way we approach the world based upon how we experienced CARE during childhood.[12]

Secure. Securely attached children have a low level of anxiety and a low level of avoidance in relationships. They are free to be themselves, knowing they have a secure base to operate from and a safe haven to return to. This leaves them feeling less anxious about their world and confident to approach their attachment figures and express their needs. They feel secure in themselves and able to manage life as a result. These children grow up being able to pay attention to the feelings of others, integrate well socially and emotionally, and value relationships.[13]

Anxious. The anxious attachment style is developed in a home in which the parent offers inconsistent or intrusive CARE. Often the parent is available or intrusive when it *is not needed* but not there consistently when he or she *is needed.* An intrusive parent might sweep into the child's room and disrupt play to force his or her own agenda without sensitivity to the transition. The inconsistent parent will miss opportunities to meet the child's attachment needs because he or she also lacks sensitivity to picking up on these clues of when the child is in need of an attachment response such as comfort, protection, or words of affirmation. In this instance a child might have been teased at school, and the parent cannot pick up on the emotional pain in order to provide a CARE response. The child is unsure of the stability of the parent in providing the CARE response needed. This instability creates an anxiety in the child around his or her own acceptance, perceiving that if he or she were more lovable, the CARE of his or her parent would be more stable.

Children raised with the anxious attachment style approach life with the belief that the world is good but they themselves are not lovable. They become preoccupied with pleasing others and drawing attention to themselves in an effort to prove they are worthy of love and attention.[14]

Avoidant. The avoidant attachment style is developed as a result of neglectful parenting. Parents who received little or no CARE themselves often repeat this cycle. We are incapable of giving something we don't have. The primary message these individuals receive is "Pull yourself up by your own bootstraps; don't depend on others." The attachment needs of these children go unmet, so they're left to their own devices. These individuals view their world as untrustworthy, and they believe the only way to survive is through self-reliance. They are high in avoidance of intimacy with others but low on anxiety, because they have given up on expecting others to be there for them. This attachment style is a major barrier to intimacy with others and leaves the individual fending for himself or herself in childhood and into adulthood.[15]

Fearful. The fearful attachment style is usually seen in children who have been physically, emotionally, or sexually abused. They find the world to be a frightening and muddled place. In this attachment style the child looks to the parent for CARE as loving parent but gets the opposite. The parent who is supposed to meet the child's attachment needs actually becomes the child's primary threat. Because their relationship has been so defined by trauma, those with this style of attachment approach life erratically and experience very unstable relationships. They sometimes cling to others and sometimes punish them with contempt or withdrawal. The result is internal instability for the individual and chaos for those around them.[16]

The Binds That Tie. Parents who are secure in their own attachment are eighty percent more likely to offer sufficient CARE responses for their own children to become securely attached. Those who have an insecure attachment style are eighty percent more likely to raise children who exhibit insecure attachment.[17] The best place for us to begin understanding our children's attachment style is to first examine our own.

Attachment and Sex

Most clinicians agree that problematic sexual behavior is often reflective of an *intimacy disorder*. All forms of intimacy, including sexual, are impacted by our attachment style and upbringing. Those with insecure attachment styles approach sexuality in ways that prevent them from experiencing a fulfilling, healthy intimacy with their spouse.[18]

Anxiously attached individuals often use sex as a way to seek approval. These individuals will give up their own sexual comfort as a means to gain the approval they long for. They will use sex as a way to pull their partner in to artificially meet their need for acceptance. Their desire for connectedness is compromised by the desire to be wanted. These individuals tend to trade true sexual intimacy for a short-term feeling of lovability.[19]

On the other hand, avoidantly attached individuals tend to use sex for self-soothing. The distorted sexual beliefs for men are rooted in avoidant attachment. Relying only on themselves to meet their attachment needs, they will *objectify* others to provide arousal experiences that meet their own needs. They tend to be singularly focused on *intensity* and are often comfortable with one-night stands and brief non-connected sex with another. Sex is not related to connection for these individuals. Like a high that can change their moods, sex is more about the *power* of being able to calm or comfort oneself at the expense of another.[20]

Individuals with a fearful attachment style approach sex as they approach life: chaotically. Sex becomes a tool used to manipulate others, or it may be avoided entirely. As was seen previously, many disorganized individuals have experienced some form of abuse. The resulting belief is that sex is traumatic and therefore bad. They may do all they can to avoid sex or will disappear into the safety of the mind—a process called *dissociation*—during intercourse. Those who use sex as a means of power and control seduce others, but only as a means of regaining power. This is an expression of their felt experience of powerlessness and internal chaos. Once again, these individuals have tremendous difficulty experiencing sex as connective.

The securely attached individual sees sex primarily as a means of emotional connection. Attachment needs of *safety, protection, comfort,* and *acceptance* are experienced both inside and outside the bedroom for securely-attached couples. They see themselves as worthy of being cared for and attuned sexually, emotionally, and spiritually. They are more aware of their own comfort level and their partner's, symbolizing the freedom to mutually give and receive in all areas of relating. This connection prevents them from being overly insecure about their bodies or their sexual performance and keeps them less concerned about these things in their partner as well. This leads to long-term sexual satisfaction and stability in the relationship. These couples recognize that their primary need is connection—not sex. Sex becomes just one of the avenues to meet their need for connection. The quality of connection experienced during intercourse allows them the freedom to deepen other areas of the relationship, such as spiritual or intellectual intimacy.

Nester or Nomad?

As it pertains to the attachment relationship, one way of understanding healthy versus unhealthy patterns of interpersonal relationship is through the lens of "nesters and nomads." At face value, there are a few distinct differences that exist between these two groups. There are also profound spiritual truths that emerge from how children negotiate these most important of interpersonal connections, truths that guide their sexual health and decision-making across the lifespan. As with most things, who you are as a parent plays a critical role in their development.

You might be asking yourself, *Exactly what are nesters and nomads anyway, and what bearing do they have on sexually healthy children?* To put this in terms of the attachment framework that we have been discussing in this chapter, a *nester* is someone who actively pursues and embodies the characteristics of secure-based attachment; a *nomad* is someone who operates in the insecure attachment styles that were previously discussed—*anxious, avoidant,* and *fearful.*

When you hear the term *nomad*, you likely think of camels, tents, and people groups who wander around the desert with their livestock. While this description is true of some nomadic tribes, the gist of the generalization is true. A *nomad* is described by Merriam-Webster as "a member of a people who have no fixed residence but move from place to place usually seasonally and within a well-defined territory; an individual who roams about."[21] The best scriptural illustration of this nomadic principle is found in the book of Exodus as Israel finds itself wandering in the desert for forty years. In Exodus, we see this cycle of forgetfulness, protest, and disengagement by Israel in its relationship with God. In essence, their nomadic experience is a social reality that is an extension of a spiritual state. Our attachment style shapes how we experience God.

Reflect on a moment when your kids were young—around three or four—and were in a situation in which they were afraid or embarrassed. How did they act or behave in these moments? Were they passive and withdrawn? Did they become angry and lash out? Did they behave in some completely unexpected way? Now think back to the description of the insecure styles of attachment that were discussed previously. Behaviors such as clinging, screaming, avoidance, emotional volatility, emotional shutdown, and an expressionless face are just a few of the presentations exhibited in insecurely attached toddlers and young children when they face situations involving strong emotion. Their relational world is one of desperation and fear, and they seek out objects, people, and things they can use to self-soothe. Now think about yourself at a similar age. Do you see in yourself something different or something identical to what you see in your children?

In every way, our parenting styles and habits are creating the attachment dynamics that our children are experiencing. As such, when we parent children in ways that cause a slide into more insecure styles of relating, we are priming them for problematic sexual behaviors later in life.

Specifically, we are allowing them to believe that (1) the parent-child relationship is an unsafe place to explore the world, including sensitive topics like sex and drugs, (2) relationships are an unsafe place to process emotion and exhibit vulnerability, and (3) self-soothing through the objectification and consumption of something external is normative, which is the exact dynamic portrayed in pornography, rape, and other forms of sexual brokenness.

When parents operate in an insecure style of attachment in the spousal relationship—where children will draw the vast majority of their truths about what it means to love, care, respect, nurture, and value themselves and others—we are actively creating a dynamic that we will later be fighting against as we try to raise sexually pure children. By persisting in our own relational brokenness, we saddle our children with an emotional debt from which it may take their lifetimes to heal. Nomads wander throughout their lives in search of this connection, often exploring possibilities that end with further emptiness—such as sex, drugs, spending, and other addictive types of behavior. They roam the relational landscape chasing the fix they haven't yet found.

I was a nomad once, foraging in the wilderness for whatever I could find that would help me ease the pain of heartbreak. Metaphorically, I was the baby robin I found in my driveway as a child who had left the nest too early: broken, cold, and dead. While this is a spiritual metaphor, it is also a reflection of my emotional state and behaviors at that time. I struggled, like the Israelites, in my ability to believe that God could or would actually be *for* me. In fact, I doubted his existence and filled my life with the fantasies of money and power I saw portrayed in the world around me, always foraging but never satisfied.

As I struggled through my late teenage years, I was called into a meeting with my youth pastor and a parent of another youth group member. Met by accusations and half-truths, I was labeled, judged, and sent on my merry way. Through my tears and screams of protest—for I did not go quietly—I relayed that I was not and would not become the person they believed me to be. The funny thing about striving *not* to become something is that we pour gasoline on the fire, quickly morphing into the thing we so strongly despise.

Within twelve months, I was more broken and lost than I had ever been—wandering, alone, and filling myself with the very things that had broken me. This is the unfortunate legacy of how the church has dealt with adolescent sexuality and sexuality in general.

Silence, as Mark Laaser states, is the greatest enemy of sexual health.[22] We parents have been silent too long, the church has been silent too long, and it is now our responsibility to correct the wrongs of good people who did not have the courage to speak health and truth in love into our lives and instead sowed shame, divisiveness, and despair.

It's easy to think, *So that's it. Game over. Brokenness and insecurity have won, and there is no hope for me or my children.* Well, not so fast.

What we see in the world of therapy is the power of a *corrective emotional experience,* or a situation in which some past hurt or injury is healed by the words and actions of a primary attachment figure. This is the biblical narrative, after all. As a parent, you have the capacity to create the greatest wounds in your children. Like it or not, it is an unavoidable truth. However, you also have the greatest capacity to heal emotional and relational injuries through facilitating corrective experiences. This is the hope we cannot lose sight of.

Take, for example, a story from my childhood. My older brother was a good student and kind-spirited fifth grader, a role model in every sense of the word—with the exception of the one time I heard him curse. At recess one day, he was assisting a student who was on the ground writhing in pain from having been kicked in a very sensitive area. The teacher on recess duty saw my brother helping this student, misattributed the cause of the pain, and put my brother "on the wall"—the equivalent to a time out.

Seeing this injustice transpire, the student who had been kicked informed the teacher that my brother was not, in fact, the guilty party. His protests, however, fell on deaf ears, and my brother was walked to "the wall."

In third grade at the time, I was busy playing with my friends when I saw it. Time seemed to stand still. There he was, my brother—my hero—"on the wall." To say I was crushed would be an understatement. I had one of those Hollywood moments where the peripheral fades away and all that can be seen is the one thing you would like to hide your eyes from. The dissonance between what I believed about my brother and the reality I was seeing became too great. I began to cry. *This is impossible,* I thought. *There must be some mistake,* my shame and my sadness suggested. *I am now the brother of a criminal,* I reasoned, somewhat melodramatically. And I remained dejected throughout the remainder of the day.

Thankfully, my parents were very engaged in our education, and when news of the scandal made it home that day, they were quick yet appropriate in moving to defend my brother's honor. While I have only my own perspective of the story to share, I have always believed that my brother's sense of self was very much protected by having my parents intervene within the school system on his behalf. They were demonstrating protection, comfort, and engagement with and for my brother, and I received a secondary gain. My own sense of right and wrong in the world was restored, my sense of justice was assuaged, and my misguided and inappropriate sense of family guilt had been washed away.

These principles of healthy attachment reached far beyond the short-term emotional implications of the experience of my brother being put "on the wall"; they reinforced a healthy understanding that the world is not against me, the people I trust and care about the most are available when I need them, and even when I can't understand why something seemingly unjust or unfair has happened, I can trust that God will provide insight and use the circumstances to grow me more in his image. In Romans 8:28 he promises us that all things work together for the good of those who love him.

The corrective experience of salvation is identical to the longing that we have to find healing in the emotional and relational wounds that we carry with us in this life. In fact, offering forgiveness and facilitating reconciliation can lead others to salvation by giving them a taste of this corrective process. Regardless of the source of the wound, we often unknowingly enter into relationships that carry with them the potential to experience the healing and completeness that had evaded us previously.

Though it has taken many years and many tears to get there, my marriage is an example of this truth. The marriage relationship, in some fashion, holds within it the potential to heal some relational hurt, wound, or disappointment that has been experienced previously. My hope is that you have found your relationship holds in it not just the *potential* for healing but also the *fullness* of healing in these corrective experiences. If that hasn't happened yet, today is the day to begin implementing these principles and experiencing the safety, trust, and acceptance that we are created to experience in the marriage relationship.

Corrective experiences bring a subtle cognitive and behavioral shift. Suddenly we are not burdened with the disappointment we have carried for so long. The hurt that was so familiar to us does not throb in the same way. We begin to experience ourselves and others as more trustworthy, more engaged, and more caring than we had been able to perceive previously. We slowly open ourselves to the possibility that we are not as broken as we believed; we are not as unacceptable as our shame has suggested.

We begin to believe there is a deeper trust, a safety, and a nurturance that we can experience in relationship. Corrective experiences birth a more secure style of relating and allow us to begin investing in the long-term good of our attachment figures and the community around us.

When my younger son was three, he was playing with friends at our house and got so wrapped up in the games that he forgot to go to the restroom. As his friends were leaving, it became clear that he was in need of hygiene assistance, so I told him to "get upstairs and get cleaned up." To my ears, it did not sound condescending or shaming, just a simple request. His experience, however, was clearly different, as evidenced by the sobs emanating from his room five minutes later.

"He was very hurt by what you said," my wife informed me. In that moment, I had a decision to make that would send ripples across the future of our relationship. It wasn't a big decision in the world's eyes, or even a hard one for me to make, but a powerfully significant one in its own right. Immersed in shame, he was in need of my acceptance and affirmation. Though I regularly communicate how proud I am of him, how good a helper he is, and how smart he is becoming, none of it mattered in that moment. In his experience, he thought that *I thought* he was dirty, unacceptable, and unwanted.

My decision was to go comfort him, providing my physical presence and validation of him. I crawled into his bed, began rubbing his back, and asked if he were crying because of what I had said. When he affirmed this, I told him how sorry I was that I had hurt his feelings and that I hadn't meant to. I asked for his forgiveness, knowing that he doesn't fully understand the theology of it all, and stayed with him until he fell asleep. I'm not a perfect father by any means, but that night I understood it in a terribly impactful way: as I am, so they will become.

Moms and dads, I don't care if your children are three, thirteen, or thirty-three—they continue needing your presence, affirmation, and modeling of what a godly life entails. Corrective experience is our responsibility in the relationship, even when they are the ones who have created the rupture. The cross is first and foremost about a repair that Christ was not responsible for. We are called to do the same. I shudder to think of the impact of that experience on my son if I had been too busy or self-absorbed to respond to my son's need.

One event doesn't ruin a child, but it plants a seed. Water that seed enough, and you will bring to life the hurt, shame, or anger that has been planted. Regardless of where you are in your life— or if you're still working out the impact of that which was planted in you during your childhood—know that we serve a God who is always willing to crawl into bed alongside us and comfort us until we are fast asleep. We need only invite him into that space.

The question that we asked at the beginning of this section is "Are you raising a nomad or a nester?" We have seen the emptiness and desolation of what we mean by *nomad* (with no offense to those people who truly are nomads in the sociological sense of the word).

On the flip side, we have this term *nester.*

One of the most incredible feats of the animal kingdom is the construction of a bird nest. The hours of time invested in gathering and assembling the necessary materials is an impressive feat in its own right. The care and intentionality demonstrated by these creatures as they prepare for the arrival of their potential offspring is quite moving. In fact, we see a similar phenomenon in mothers who are about to welcome their own offspring into the world—painting the walls just the right shade, arranging the furniture just-so, selecting and hanging the right decorations. It is a monumentally important task of mothers-to-be to spend these hours planning and preparing so that they are physically and emotionally prepared to welcome their little bundle of joy into the world. In this process, we see nesting demonstrated in the truest sense of the word.

While a vast array of differences exists between species, there is certainly a parallel to be drawn between these two forms of nesting behaviors that are exhibited by each. At the core, there is an instinctual drive toward preparing to welcome offspring into the world. Hormones do their important work of guiding the energy and vision of mothers-to-be as they finalize their living space to create a space of safety, comfort, and nurturance for their new additions.

For us as a species, however, we have more than an animalistic drive toward offering these relational dynamics; we have a relational and spiritual connection that exists beyond what creatures in the animal kingdom are able to embody. We have the capacity to anticipate, to dream, and to believe. These bonds of connection are forged and maintained in relationship.

As God reveals himself to us through the creation narrative, he communicates himself as a very social being. In Genesis 1:26 he states, "Let us make mankind in our image, in our likeness." We see from the beginning of our understanding of God as he reveals himself that there is a relational quality demonstrated within the Trinity. In fact, his relational essence is revealed at the moment of creating humanity, suggesting that there is a relational element of himself that is characterized by humanity's relationship to him and ultimately in humans' relationship to one another, as we see in Christ's words in Matthew 25:34-40:

> Then the King will say to those on his right, "Come, you who are blessed by my Father; take your inheritance, the kingdom prepared for you since the creation of the world. For I was hungry and you gave me something to eat, I was thirsty

and you gave me something to drink, I was a stranger and you invited me in, I needed clothes and you clothed me, I was sick and you looked after me, I was in prison and you came to visit me."

Then the righteous will answer him, "Lord, when did we see you hungry and feed you, or thirsty and give you something to drink? When did we see you a stranger and invite you in, or needing clothes and clothe you? When did we see you sick or in prison and go to visit you?"

The King will reply, "Truly I tell you, whatever you did for one of the least of these brothers and sisters of mine, you did for me."

In large measure, this nesting instinct is different in us as human beings due to its function as a spiritual process. Yes, it is a physical and emotional process, but it is also imbued with the characteristics that we see depicted in God's interaction with Israel throughout the history of the Old Testament, as well as Christ's engagement with the social world in the New Testament.

These attachment principles are evidenced throughout the scriptural narrative in ways that are often misunderstood. Where some see wrath, God is providing protection. Where some see judgment, he is offering invitation and acceptance. Where some read punishment, God is providing presence. When we begin to understand scripture through an attachment framework, we are more able to fully understand how it is that God works in the life of Israel.

We also begin to understand the notion of *nester* on a deeper level. As parents, we are called to embody the secure base and safe haven Christ has modeled for us. When we provide curiosity, accessibility, responsiveness, and engagement, we lay the foundation for healthy sexuality in our children; but more important, we lay the foundation for them to experience God as he truly is and themselves as they truly are. They experience God when we meet their needs of protection, comfort, affirmation, and safety in healthy ways. I can think of no greater gift to give our children than an accurate understanding of who God is, who he has created them to be, and where sex fits into the big picture of their lives.

Section Three

THE FINER POINTS
STARTING "THE
CONVERSATION"

eight
START
"THE CONVERSATION"

S o you have all of this great information—now how do you use it? The first has to do with timing. The fact is, you and I have a responsibility to engage our children in a very proactive fashion. We know that diet and exercise are critical to growing healthy children. We don't let them eat whatever they want; we don't let them play in the street; we don't let them run with scissors. Yet when it comes to their sexual health, our lack of comfort or confidence in facilitating "the conversation" leaves our children fending for themselves. When we leave children and adolescents to choose for themselves, many of them will choose that which brings them the most pleasure. If timing is critical in raising sexually healthy children, the best time to begin "the conversation" is now.

Another issue has to do with competence. One of the themes you probably have already identified in this book is that to grow sexually healthy children, we must also be sexually healthy ourselves—or at least on the path toward sexual wellness. Most of the teenagers I have worked with in a clinical context are very perceptive to any level of discomfort I exhibit. Some will use this discomfort as an opportunity to actively change the topic, avoiding "the conversation" altogether. Others will act like a deer in the headlights: mention the word *sex*, and they freeze where they sit. In flight mode, they become flooded with fear, guilt, and discomfort and will act weird for weeks to follow. And I am just their therapist—not their parent.

Knowing that these possible responses exist when you do not present as confident and prepared, the right time to begin "the conversation" is when you have a game plan that you are comfortable with—called *structure* in the model presented below. When participating in "the conversation" as a team, it is critical that you and your spouse be on the same page.

Negotiating who will cover what topics is essential. For example, it is important that fathers be the ones who talk with their boys about male sexual issues. Likewise, mothers need to be the ones discussing menarche, the menstrual cycle, and other feminine topics.

Perfect Timing

With anything in life, clear communication is essential. I discovered this principle the hard way one afternoon while visiting my wife's grandparents in Texas. Having just completed a whirlwind tour of pre-doctoral internship interviews from Dallas to Houston, we elected to spend some time visiting her family outside Austin. My body, exhausted from the demands of traveling and interviewing, protested my overly demanding schedule by becoming sick. My wife's grandmother, the most nurturing soul I have ever had the pleasure of meeting, brought me two tablets and instructed me to take them. With vivid memories of eating antacid tablets at my grandparents' house when I was younger, I eagerly consumed the tablets and waited for relief to come. And boy did it ever! Within fifteen seconds I was foaming at the mouth like a rabid dog and throwing up everything I had eaten in the past three days. Apparently effervescent tablets are meant to dissolve in a glass of water, not the stomach.

The lack of communication that transpired, fueled by my previous experiences and misperception, created a situation that was most unpleasant. As parents, our best intentions often put us in a similar predicament. Our care and concern for our children move us to provide information that can be of assistance to their sexual and spiritual health. However, our lack of clarity in communication sees them unintentionally misuse the very thing that was intended to help them. When it comes to sex, your natural inclination might be to tell them just the body parts and their functions without ever explaining how it all works on a relational level. This chapter is designed to assist you in facilitating a more detailed conversation.

As a parent there are several roles and responsibilities we will have to fulfill. Activities such as teaching a son manners or teaching a daughter to act like a lady are just a couple of these responsibilities. These are acts of parental stewardship. Helping our children learn that striking out is part of the game and that sometimes our friends say mean things about us become important developmental processes that help them understand life on a deeper level.

While these conversations come somewhat easily for us, conversations about sexuality do not. The act of sexual stewardship for our children has gone overlooked in many Christian circles, not due to a lack of awareness of the need but rather from an excessive fear of what might happen if our children know about sex. It is "Killer Bee Syndrome."

We develop an irrational fear about something that serves a very important function, avoiding it at all costs to us while unknowingly exacting a huge toll on our children. What we see as an act of protection unknowingly leaves our children vulnerable to the influences of their social world and peer groups. Having a model to guide us through these murky waters is essential.

START "the Conversation"

This is where the START model comes in. Specifically, this model will help you understand the importance of dynamics such as the timing and location of each conversation, known as *structure*; the importance of being *truthful* in these conversations; how to remain *accessible* when your children have questions or need more information; the power of *responsive* parenting; and a *thorough* review of important points for your children to know about sex and sexuality.

Structure defines the *who, what, why, when,* and *where* of "the conversation" about sex you will be facilitating with your children. One of the critical acts of stewarding our children's sexuality is answering who is going to address what, explain why that is, and deciding when and where to have this most important of talks. You and your spouse must agree upon when will be the right time to teach your child about their bodies and eventually why people have sexual intercourse. As you can imagine, this changes with the ages and stages your children are in.

Rick Cicchetti provides a review of Mark Laaser's recommendations about what to address at each stage.

Infancy and Toddler (0-3 years):[1] During training the child to go to the bathroom, begin teaching the child the correct names of body parts. Between the age of two and three it is very common for children to touch their genitals and begin exploring bodily sensations. If a child receives positive support and healthy boundaries, he or she is more likely to be independent and self-assured. In this stage of development children learn about the differences in gender. Lack of early affirmation can lead to internalized confusion and sexual identity problems in later life.

Childhood (4-9 years):[2] This is a time for children to learn about safe boundaries and for you to discuss and teach about private areas of the body while affirming their curiosity. Explain the parts of the body and discuss the basic biology of sex, reproduction, and intercourse as a picture of how God created us to become one flesh with our spouse. Help your children begin to manage their bodily functions as an early act of self-care. Teach them how to honestly express emotions. Make them aware of healthy coping strategies such as talking things out, and unhealthy coping strategies such as sexual behaviors or substance use.

Helping children develop friendships is vital during this period of development, including platonic and male-female social relationships and friendships as well as appropriate social boundaries. If they begin using technology during these years, be sure to implement the appropriate software as well as educating them about Internet safety.

It is critical that children understand the following messages during this period of development:

- It is never okay for anyone to touch your private parts.
- It is never okay for anyone to ask you to touch his or her private parts.
- It is never okay for anyone to see you or ask you to see him or her naked.
- It is never okay for anyone to ask you to be sexual with someone while he or she watches.

119

If anyone asks you to do these things, leave immediately. If you need to yell for help, do so. Anything you are asked to keep secret should be told to Mommy or Daddy right away. Helping children grasp God's role in creation and sexuality can be taught during these years.

Puberty (10-14 years):[3] This is a time when children will be experiencing tremendous biological changes. During these years a parent's job is to validate, validate, validate. If parents have not discussed sexual maturation and biological changes with children, it can be a very confusing time. Important parent/child interactions during these years include making sure children have a full understanding about sex, the process, conception, and childbirth; regularly affirming them physically, emotionally, and mentally; touching them in nonsexual, loving ways; providing them with biblical, moral boundaries while not overreacting to the mistakes associated with experimentation; making them aware of symptoms of problem sexual behaviors; being ready to discuss issues and myths related to pornography and cultural sexuality—and getting them help as needed.

Encourage them to have healthy friendships and celebrate their transition into adulthood. Provide them with opportunities to be trusted Christian mentors, and continue to foster their spiritual development during these years.

Adolescence (15-19 years):[4] During this period of development, conversations about sexual abstinence before marriage, spirituality, and staying pure in a sexualized culture should be the main topics. Our primary tasks as parents include continuing to have conversations with our children while allowing them to be more in control of the dialogue; teaching them about specific sexual behaviors and problems; modeling healthy thinking, behavior, and communication; and continuing to affirm them in all aspects of their lives. You will need to continue to set safe boundaries for your children, although they will need to be active participants in co-creating these boundaries. Encourage them to be spiritually and socially active, and remain aware of any behavioral problems or unhealthy patterns of relating that you see. Challenge them with spiritual vision, and always model God's grace.

Before approaching your children, determine what their individual limitations are as far as comprehending content, level of mental fatigue, and current emotional state. Tacking "the conversation" on at the end of a long day of exams and orthodontist appointments is certainly not recommended.

In addition, you must know what your limitations are, as you examined in the first chapter. It is necessary that you are mentally present and emotionally available to talk to your children about sex. Remember to CARE. A crowded restaurant at the end of a long and stressful week is not optimal for anyone, especially the child. Maybe you and your spouse both want to be present. Whatever you decide, find an activity that you and your children can engage in together while facilitating "the conversation." Activities such as playing a game, doing outdoor activities, eating dinner, or practicing driving are all open windows of opportunity for you to speak truth into their lives. You know them best. Find the activity that best suits them, and take a leap of faith.

In order for children to accept what you're teaching them, approach the task with a calm and direct attitude. Kids smell fear like sharks smell blood. Just one drop, and you're lunch! One way to calm your nerves is to create a written outline that you can refer to during the discussion with your child. The outline should be age-appropriate with the intent to educate the child at his or her developmental level. As stated previously, this is an ongoing conversation, not a one-shot talk. Being able to approach your child with a positive attitude will bring about a healthy and successful discussion. You understand your child's attention span, so you need to decide if this conversation will be one session or multiple exchanges with time for questions and answers.

Young children might be inclined to make sense of the information you provide through exploratory play. This is normal and healthy as long as there are boundaries in place—like not allowing Bobby to play doctor with Sally from next door.

As kids mature and experience puberty, it is best to allow for multiple points of contact over a window of time and to be available for questions they might have. You may find their questions interesting, funny—maybe even thought-provoking. The patience you are able to demonstrate in talking with your child will benefit him or her in understanding the sex talk topic and the importance for him or her to listen. Failure to take the necessary time to approach the sex conversation in a patient and calm matter may deter the child from focusing on the words you're speaking.

You don't have to get it all done in just one sitting. You and your child would both be overwhelmed if you even tried. So take the time to speak and listen, and don't waiver from your goal of educating your child. If you have more than one child, talking with the oldest may have a trickle-down effect with other siblings. Address what your oldest child will discuss, and tell his brothers and sisters in language that fits their developmental stage.

Truthfulness is the next step in the START model. The old adage states, "The truth hurts." During some point in "the conversation" you will become uncomfortable, perhaps when your child is five—or maybe thirteen. If you could already describe the reproductive cycle to your twelve-year-old without blushing, you would not be taking the time to read this book. You might be uncomfortable using the words and describing the behaviors, but at some point your kids are going to need this information. Regardless of when this discomfort happens, be honest with your children.

Tell them the truth about their bodies, about what the Bible says about sex, and even about your own sexual past, depending on their age. Also, when things get uncomfortable, be sure to talk about what is happening between you and your child. By exhibiting vulnerability and taking ownership for your personal embarrassment, you are laying the foundation for continuing "the conversation" by protecting your child from personalizing the shame or discomfort he or she perceives. Humor is a great tool to use in these situations. Being able to collect your thoughts and generate a different plan of approach can enable you to take a better approach to the topic. What is critical is that you do not allow an awkward conversation to go unprocessed. If you do, you send the message that sex is too uncomfortable to talk about, that you have no idea what you're talking about, and that they're on their own in figuring out this whole sex thing.

When it comes to the truth, most children are perceptive and can read your body language, although you may not know it. In your mind you may see yourself as the epitome of cool—your poker face is unreadable. You may not realize in the moment that you're leaking your thoughts and reactions in the conversations with your children. If you roll your eyes, change your tone of voice, or alter your facial expressions, your children will pick up on it quickly. This may be an indication to them that you aren't listening, may not be taking them seriously, or aren't happy with them. They begin to wrongly assume that whatever you are leaking is somehow about them. Again, shame has its roots in relational experience. Don't plant it unnecessarily in your children's lives. Even if it means practicing in front of a mirror, make sure you take steps to manage the "leakage" that may show up.

You can be prepared, rehearse what you're going to say to your child—and in the middle of the discussion your child asks the question "Mom, did you have sex before you were married to

Dad?" If you're like any other adult—parent or not—you'll find yourself reeling unless you're prepared for spontaneous questions like this. This is not an uncommon question for most children to ask. They're curious about the subject, they look to you as a role model, and they often ask the unexpected. If they do, your response must be to keep your cool and not lose control of the situation. If you show any kind of regression or emotional outburst, younger children will assume they did something wrong, while older kids are more likely to become dismissive of you.

Keep calm and carry on in the face of unexpected and uncomfortable queries. The best plan of action for this situation is to expect the unexpected. If you have adhered to structure, you will have a response prepared that addresses the areas of your own story that are easily understood by your child at his or her age.

These questions are more likely to occur with older children. However, if you wait until children are of an age where they already understand sex and the purpose for it, you have likely missed an open window and will have some additional work to do in the area of restoring sexual health. They have heard "truth" elsewhere. The older the children the more inquisitive and detailed they will probably be, given the increased likelihood of exposure to sexual content. They most likely have exposure to the term "sex" but do not typically understand boundaries. They figure you are fair game. If you're telling them what sex is all about, they may turn it into a rapid succession of questions about your morality and behavior when you were their age.

Remember: you are their role model. Curiosity about what Mom and Dad do and how often is developmentally appropriate and needs to be responded to honestly. Being able to explain your life and what you have learned along the journey goes a long way in helping them make good choices. These questions are normal and should be anticipated, and the more prepared you are, the better job you can do of providing them with an honest and helpful answer.

One big fear is that if we talk honestly to our children about taboo things, we're giving them permission or planting a curiosity to explore it. Providing structure by setting boundaries for your child is an aspect that cannot be overlooked; truthfulness without boundaries is traumatic. You must explain to the child why you're discussing this subject, and now that you've had this talk, what is permissible and what is not.

Likewise, in later adolescent years there may be opportunities for them to become sexually active. These opportunities do not mean they have permission to participate in the behavior, and this needs to be made clear. Talking honestly equips them to make good choices in the moment rather than simply acting on impulse. They need to understand the appropriate time within God's design for human sexuality to fully engage, explore, and enjoy the gift of sex. We need to model for and communicate directly to our children the fact that sexual acting out impacts all parties involved, including the families.

Accessibility. So you implemented your structure, told the truth—the whole truth and nothing but the truth. Now what? Some kids take longer to process the information than others. Let them have their space.

Younger children, inquisitive creatures that they are, may come to you and ask, "Where do babies come from?"—especially in light of a pregnant parent or aunt. Most parents are introduced to the world of sex education by their children's curiosity, including yours truly. Children ask this question from a place of innocence. It is a sign of healthy curiosity if they come to you with their questions. If your child asks you this question, your first response and your demeanor will indicate whether or not it was an appropriate question to ask you. Take a deep breath, understand where the question comes from, and have a thoughtful response prepared.

Validate your children's curiosity about life and the emotion they are feeling in anticipating the baby's pending arrival, but also use it as an opportunity to teach them about their own bodies. A great example for a toddler would be "That is a very good question, sweetie. I know how excited/nervous/curious you are about the baby being born. God has given mommies and daddies body parts to help make a baby. The baby grows in Mommy's belly until it is ready to be born." For a child who is a little older, you can give a little more truthful information about conception and pregnancy and birth. When you lay a foundation of structure and truthfulness, you are more accessible to your children.

With all sex talks, there is the chance for a humorous follow-up question. Sometimes these come at unexpected times, so stay on your toes. Answering harshly or dodging the question plants the seeds of shame. Accessibility suggests you are approachable, prepared, and ready to answer to their questions. You will very likely be flooded with a variety of thoughts and emotions that range anywhere from shame to fear to relief. Regardless of what is happening on the inside, keep your body language, tone of voice, and facial expressions cool, calm, and collected.

Responsiveness. To say I did not handle my teenage years well would be a bit of an understatement. I did not go as far off the deep end as some, but I can say that I went off farther than I ever intended to—and farther than I ever want to go again. After high school graduation and one year after being shamed and wounded by accusations from a youth pastor and a teen sponsor in the church, I hit rock bottom.

I had always wondered what it would be like to be on the inside of a building as it was imploding. I found out. On the worst night of my life, I found my way into my father's bedroom and asked him if he could come talk to me. I broke down weeping as I shared the decisions I had been making in my life and where they had put me. We sat on a loveseat in a dark living room at two o'clock in the morning, and I sobbed uncontrollably into my dad's chest. There was no judgment; he already knew. There was no condemnation, no shaming, and no "I told you so." He knew that I knew better, and his heart broke with mine. As I poured out my hurt and my brokenness, he did exactly what a dad should do for his son: he held me tightly and told me we would get through it together. The process of finding healing and grace started that night on the loveseat, in the dark at two A.M. I would not be who I am today without that corrective experience.

With that story in mind, a few things about responsiveness are important to remember. First, teaching your child about sex is a progressive journey that will take time and will be accomplished as they develop. Letting them know you are available to talk at every stage, even when it seems that you're the last person on earth they would want to talk to, plants the seeds of connection. I didn't seek out my father on a whim. He had planted seeds of safety and trust earlier in my life that let me come to him in my moment of utmost vulnerability. When I needed him most, he moved quickly to help address my emotional and spiritual pain.

Second, you must know that every child will turn at some point in his or her life to friends for information and advice, especially during later adolescence and teenage years. You will be replaced—period. However, you must also realize that your input carries far greater weight than you can imagine. When the crisis moments come, you will be needed. And when you are needed, you must be ready to respond to your child with compassion. The child already knows he or she has made a mistake; he or she is coming to you for help in picking up the broken pieces. When you establish yourself as a positive influence in your child's life, you create a stronger avenue for you to talk to your child about sex, health, and relationships.

Third, responsiveness is a proactive process. Seek out your children. Be curious about what is happening in their lives and the challenges they are facing at school. Being a proactive parent means you inform your children about human sexuality before life does. As stated earlier, teaching your children about body parts and their functions is a basic responsibility. As your child matures, so should the specificity of information and wisdom you convey to them. Each discussion teaches them a little more. And be sure to give yourself a break. You can't possibly know it all, but you can be responsive by investigating and answering questions as they come up.

We all want what is best for our kids. We cringe when they wreck their bikes, but we realize that it's an unavoidable part of the learning process. Sex operates differently. Keep sex a subject that you're always learning about and talking about with your children. And when they wreck—because somewhere along the way they will—make sure you're there, willing to do whatever it takes to help them grow, learn, and heal through it.

Be **thorough.** The last component of the START model has to do with the thoroughness of information that you share with your kids. While it would be easy to inundate them with far too much information, it is important that you be mindful of the developmental stages identified previously. It's important that kids be engaged on an appropriate developmental level; often they are more capable of understanding—and likely more experienced—than we would like to believe. Content from this book can be a great conversation-starter.

Each of the points listed below will sound different based on the age and development of the child, as well as other variables, such as birth order, gender, and so on. Addressing each of these points, as well as the unexpected dynamics that emerge, is an essential part of stewarding our children's sexuality. Larry Daly provides ten insights for parents to provide a thorough sex education.[5]

1. Teach your child the names of his or her body parts, using appropriate labels, not nicknames. If your child uses a nickname, be sure the child understands the body part he or she has named.

2. Discuss the functions of these body parts. Most parts of our genitalia serve multiple purposes, so inform them of the difference in parts and uses.

3. Identify for your child healthy and unhealthy types of touch. The same innocent touch at three becomes something very different at seven.

4. Teach your child *whom* he or she can touch, *where* he or she can touch the person, and explain *why*.

5. Inform your child that all questions are appropriate when it comes to sex. Keeping the lines of communication open is critical to stewarding your child's sexuality.

6. Teach your child that there will be sexual urges from time to time, and explain to the child how to deal with these urges. Explain that they are our body's response to being attracted to someone. Help them understand that urges do not have to become impulses.

7. Talk to your child about self-control as his or her body begins to develop biological reactions, urges, sensations, and feelings during puberty and beyond. Discuss with older kids that distraction methods such as prayer, a phone call, a cold shower, going on a run, and so forth can be helpful.

8. Inform your child of the necessary boundaries to adhere to when touch becomes an issue during adolescence and teenage years. Explain that peers may want to sexually explore

his or her body and the need to be safe and how to guard himself or herself from being inappropriately touched.

9. Teach your child how to respond to inappropriate sexual touching, that no one is to touch him or her sexually, and that he or she should report this touching to you or an authority figure he or she can trust. Urge that if someone tries to touch or does touch him or her not to wait to tell. If you aren't available, have the child tell the individual who is in charge of him or her. It is important that your child knows that he or she has a safe alternative and will be protected.

10. Teach your child that as he or she grows older and his or her environment changes, peers may invite or try to force participation in inappropriate sexual experiences from viewing pornography to forced sexual acts. Inform your child that he or she is to bring these situations to your immediate attention.

These ten steps form a foundational approach to keeping your children healthy spiritually, emotionally, and socially. As they mature, they will more fully understand why God gave them each body part and the need to have it. Also, these ten areas address safety issues that can help keep children from becoming victims of sexual perpetration.

It can feel intimidating to begin the process of talking to our kids about sex. By having a place to START "the conversation," you are equipping your children to develop healthy habits and fulfilling your role as a steward of their sexuality and innocence. Parents receive no higher calling than that.

Restoration Hardware: Three Nails and a Cross

When sexual mistakes hit home, there is no snapping of the fingers to make the problem go away. There are no quick tricks or magical potions that will undo the error that has been committed. Several individuals need to participate in the healing process: you, your child, your spouse, and depending on the circumstances, siblings and others who were involved in the behavior. Pastoral insight and professional counseling are also recommended avenues for healing.

Ten Guidelines for Sexual Restoration

1. **Identify the elephant in the room.** You and your spouse need to get to the root of the problem. Ignoring your children's problematic sexual behavior will only make it more difficult for everyone in the long run. You need to present a unified front in addressing the behavior and stay in constant communication with one another about how things are progressing. Do not let yourselves become divided over how you decide to address the issue.

2. **Keep things simple.** All children will make mistakes and will deal with their mistakes differently, including emotionally, mentally, and physically. When they understand they are responsible for the situation, they will have shame and guilt to work through. Your affirmation that they are fundamentally good—but made a bad decision—will keep them from over-identifying with the shame and keep them from long-term struggles in this area. Complex plans sound good in theory but are unsustainable and ultimately doomed to fail. The simple path often leads to success.

3. **Include your kids in the solution-building process.** Kids need to be active participants in restoring their lives back to normalcy. As a parent, you can lay out a plan for them that is simple and easy to follow. Much like the START model, restoration begins with providing them

more structure in the form of rules and consequences. Tying these rules and consequences to the behavior is essential, such as removing all screen time—use of phones, computers, televisions, handheld gaming devices—when the issue is online pornography or "sexting." If certain other people are contributing to the problem, work with your kids on how those relationships need to change in order for the process to be effective.

4. **Adopt a need-to-know basis.** Everyone in the family must be on board and participate in the restoration process. If you have an older sibling who has no problem with giving your child access to his or her computer so he or she can surf the Internet for pornography, the structure unravels quickly. Restoration is not the child's responsibility; it is the entire family's responsibility. Everyone needs to be on the same page, but it is not always necessary to spill the beans and provide details to the other children about why the structure exists. If one individual in the family is hindering the healing process, he or she will need to be positively coached to follow the restoration plan, including any safeguards that have been identified.

5. **Get all hands on deck.** Talk with pastors, teachers, babysitters, and anyone else who regularly interacts with the child. Coach them in providing empathy, but also encourage them to monitor the child's behavior. Accountability is a critical component of changing habits. Even without knowing all of the gory details, those who have a vested interest in your child's life can greatly assist in the healing process.

6. **Hit the ground running.** There is no designated time frame of how long restoration will take. However, your child's behavior needs to be addressed on a daily basis

until his or her habits are curtailed or the behavior ultimately ceases. Make this a priority so your child does not suffer longer than necessary. The restoration process should not take a year in most cases. If the behavior is identified early and the proper resources are utilized, the behavior will change over a short period of time.

7. **Stay connected.** Sit down on a weekly basis and discuss the progress your child has made. This is a chance to stay on each other's radar, make any necessary tweaks to the restoration process, or set benchmarks for restoring privileges. As milestones are reached, celebrate the accomplishments. Failing to give credit where it is due can undermine the process of restoration. These meetings can be spaced out as continued success is achieved. Be sure to validate both successful changes as well as effort to change.

8. **Pay attention to the warning signs.** Warning signs need to be addressed immediately during the restoration process. Time spent in isolation, changes in behavior, erratic behavior, changes in sleeping patterns, and thoughts of injury to self or another should all be taken very seriously. The family and friends who are dealing with the restoration process know your child the best. Trust your intuition, even if it creates frustration in your child. You can work through a false positive where your child is kept safe rather than asking yourself what you could have done differently in the event of a tragedy.

9. **Two steps forward, one step back.** Be prepared for the failures in the restoration process. Chances are your child will not instantly jump into line and change his or her behavior. If so, you have likely caught the behavior very early, which is a good thing. Patience is a virtue, and you will have to work through these ruptures with grace and

understanding. When the consequences are outlined and previously agreed upon, the road is much smoother. If a relapse happens, be sure to help your child explore what precipitated the event, what was happening as the behavior was being engaged in, and what the child is learning about himself or herself as a result.

10. **Forgiveness.** This is the most important aspect of the restoration process. There is no restoration without forgiveness. You must voice to your child that he or she is forgiven. Help the child work on embracing forgiveness for himself or herself as well as seeking forgiveness from those he or she has hurt or providing forgiveness to those who have hurt him or her. Daily devotions and prayer are essential in forgiveness becoming a defining part of the child's restoration process. The journey is not just a physical and emotional one—it is fundamentally a spiritual one.

Restoration is the work of grace in our lives. We serve a God who longs to restore in us the fullness of his image, *Imago Dei*. As parents, we become co-participants in this process of reclaiming the image of God for our children. This process is best detailed in the Zephaniah 3, where we see God actively facilitating restoration in the remnant of Israel. Secure attachment is depicted through God's orientation to his children in this passage. The beautiful words we find serve as both a comfort and a promise as you begin the process of stewarding your children's sexuality:

The Lord your God is with you, the Mighty Warrior who saves. He will take great delight in you; in his love he will no longer rebuke you, but will rejoice over you with singing. (Zephaniah 3:17)

These words detail God's promise regarding who he will be in our lives. He loves us. He protects us. He delights in us. He nurtures us. He rejoices over us with singing. He is our rock and our fortress, our secure base and our safe haven. Let us go and embody these truths in the lives of our children. Their souls and their sexuality depend on it.

NOTES

Chapter 1

1. W. M. Struthers, *Wired for Intimacy: How Pornography Hijacks the Male Brain* (Downers Grove, Ill.: InterVarsity Press, 2009), 33.

2. J. R. Stoner, *The Social Costs of Pornography: A Collection of Papers* (Princeton, N.J.: Witherspoon Institute, 2010), 14.

3. R. Caniglia, "Counselor: Average age for first viewing of pornography is 11-years-old <http://www.ktiv.com/story/21230061/2013/02/18/the-age-at-which-youth-view-inappropriate-images-may-shock-you?utm_source=twitter&utm_medium=social&utm_content=57abcd50-4f78-4e4d-851f-673120da250>.

4. G. R. Hanson, P. J. Venturelli, and A. E. Fleckenstein, *Drugs and Society*, ninth ed. (Sudbury, Mass.: Jones and Bartlett Publishers, 2005), 364.

5. D. J. Siegel and T. P. Bryson, *The Whole-Brain Child* (New York: Delacarte Press, 2011), 27.

Chapter 2

1. Siegel and Bryson, *The Whole-Brain Child,* 22.

2. Stoner, *The Social Costs of Pornography,* 14.

3. J. Grohol, "11 Surprising Facts about America's Sexual Behaviors," *Psych Central* <http://psychcentral.com/blog/archives/2010/10/06/11-surprising-facts-about-americas-sexual-behaviors/>.

4. Author unknown, "Study Suggests Young Are Delaying Marriage Because of Rising College Debt," *HuffPost College* <http://www.huffingtonpost.com/2012/03/28/study-college-debt-marriage-loans-rates-rising_n_1385548.html>.

5. M. C. Ferree, *No Stones: Women Redeemed from Sexual Addiction* (Downers Grove, Ill.: InterVarsity Press, 2010), 40.

6. Stoner, *The Social Costs of Pornography,* 15.

Chapter 3

1. ANI, "5 Myths About Male Sexuality," *The Mid-Day* <http://www.mid-day.com/relationships/2011/aug/030811-5-myths-about-male-sexuality.htm>.

2. Ibid.

3. Struthers, *Wired for Intimacy,* 105.

4. Ibid., 102.

Chapter 4

1. Ashley, "Sex Myths About Women" <http://shine.yahoo.com/love-sex/sex-myths-about-women-1384933.html>.

2. E. Monk-Turner and C. Purcell, "Sexual Violence in Pornography: How Prevalent Is It?" *Gender Issues,* 1999 <http://link.springer.com/article/10.1007%2Fs12147-999-0015-7?LI=true#page-1>.

3. Stoner, *The Social Costs of Pornography,* 60-61.

4. Ibid., 60.

5. L. Segal, "Pornography and Violence: What the 'Experts' Really Say," *Feminist Review,* 1999 <http://www.jstor.org/discover/10.2307/1395107?uid=2&uid=4&sid=21101904448143>.

6. American Psychological Association Task Force, "Sexualization of Girls," 2007 <http://www.apa.org/pi/women/programs/girls/report.aspx>.

7. S. Biddulph, "The Corruption of a Generation: Our Daughters Are Facing Sexualisation from Primary School Age," *The Daily Mail* <http://www.dailymail.co.uk/femail/article-2264781/Corrupting-generation-In-new-major-Mail-series-renowned-psychologist-Steve-Biddulph-argues-daughters-facing-unprecedented-crisis.html>.

8. Ferree, *No Stones,* 40.

9. Ibid., 35

10. Author unknown, "Sex-for-Sale Statistics," *Beauty from Ashes* <http://beautyfromashes.org/contentpages.aspx?parentnavigationid=0&viewcontentpageguid=3293b02d-f447-4afe-a0be-f120fc8471b4>.

Chapter 5

1. Grohol, "11 Surprising Facts about America's Sexual Behaviors."

2. Ibid.

3. Stoner, *The Social Costs of Pornography,* 72.

4. Ibid., 4.

5. Author unknown, "Children Watching YouTube Are 'Three Clicks' Away from Explicit Material," *The Telegraph,* February 5, 2013 <http://www.telegraph.co.uk/technology/internet/9849267/Children-watching-YouTube-are-three-clicks-away-from-explicit-material.html?utm_source=twitter&utm_medium=social&utm_content=84d527e1-3c48-497a-b81a-0493a6c4dbcf>.

6. D. Finkelhor, C. Sabina, and J. Wolak, "The Nature and Dynamics of Internet Pornography Exposure to Youth," *CyberPsychology & Behavior,* 11(6), 2008, 1-3.

7. J. McDowell and D. McDowell, *Straight Talk with Your Kids About Sex* (Eugene, Oreg.: Harvest House Publishers, 2012), 9.

8. M. Allen, D. D'Alessio, and K. Brezgei, "A Meta-Analysis Summarizing the Effects of Pornography II: Aggression After Exposure," Health Communications Research, 1995, 22:258-83.

9. Finkelhor et al., "The Nature and Dynamics of Internet Pornography Exposure to Youth."

10. Larry Daly, personal correspondence.

11. Stoner, *The Social Costs of Pornography,* 72.

12. Author unknown, "Teenage Sexting Statistics," *PCs N Dreams* <http://www.pcsndreams.com/Pages/Sexting_Statistics.html>.

13. Author unknown, "Kids View Porn and 'Sexts' as Mundane," *LondonderrySentinel*<http://www.londonderrysentinel.co.uk/news/local/kids-view-porn-and-sexts-as-mundane-1-4753238?utm_source=twitter&utm_medium=social&utm_content=ebb169be-094d-46b3-821d-9377c308f d2f>.

14. Author unknown, "Teen Porn: The Risky New Trend for a Fame-Seeking Generation" <http://antipornographyactivist.wordpress.com/2013/02/06/teen-porn-the-risky-new-trend-for-a-fame-seeking-generation-home-made-pornography-created-and-distributed-by-teens-of-teens/>.

15. R. Weiss, "Sex, Tech and the Addiction Epidemic," *Counselor Magazine* <http://www.counselormagazine.com/detailpage.aspx?pageid=1443&Lang Type=1033&id=6442451102>.

16. Author unknown, "Non-Technical Measures to Protect Kids Online," Internet Safety 101 <http://internetsafety101.org/InternetSafetyrules.htm>.

17. Grohol, "11 Surprising Facts about America's Sexual Behaviors."

18. D. D. Cowell, "Autoerotic Asphyxiation: Secret Pleasure—Lethal Outcome?" *Pediatrics: Official Journal of the American Academy of Pediatrics* <http://pediatrics.aappublications.org/content/124/5/1319.full>.

19. Grohol, "11 Surprising Facts about America's Sexual Behaviors."

20. M. Downs, "4 Things You Didn't Know About Oral Sex," *WebMD* <http://www.webmd.com/sex-relationships/features/4-things-you-didnt-know-about-oral-sex>.

21. S. Murphy, "40% of Teens Video Chat with Their Friends," *Pew Internet & American Life Project* <http://www.pewinternet.org/Media-Mentions/2012/Teens-Video-Chat-With-Their-Friends.aspx>.

22. Author unknown, "Youth Pledge," Internet Safety 101 <http://internetsafety101.org/InternetSafetyrules.htm>.

23. N. Burgert, "Addicted to Pinterest: 4 Reasons Why Social Media Age Limits Matter." *KC Kids Doc Contemporary Parenting* <http://kckidsdoc.com/social-media-age-limit.html>.

24. Stoner, *The Social Costs of Pornography,* 17.

25. D. Boone, *A Charitable Discourse: Talking About the Things That Divide Us* (Kansas City: Beacon Hill Press of Kansas City, 2010), 133.

26. American Psychological Association, "Child Sexual Abuse: What Parents Should Know" <http://www.apa.org/pi/families/resources/child-sexual-abuse.aspx>.

27. American Psychological Association Task Force, "Sexualization of Girls."

28. Ibid.

29. S. McClurg, "How to Monitor Apps on Your Child's Device" <http://www.covenanteyes.com/2013/02/13/how-to-monitor-apps-on-your-childs-device/?utm_source=twitter&utm_medium=social&utm_content=e54b0f24-2443-4081-a285-3d3a34dfcc15>.

Chapter 6

1. Daly, personal correspondence.
2. Laurie Heap, personal correspondence.
3. Ibid.
4. Ibid.
5. Ibid.
6. Ibid.
7. Ibid.
8. Ibid.
9. Mark Hayse, personal correspondence.

Chapter 7

1. Todd Frye, personal correspondence.
2. Ibid.
3. Ibid.
4. Ibid.
5. Ibid.
6. S. Johnson, *Hold Me Tight: Seven Conversations for a Lifetime of Love* (New York: Little, Brown and Company, 2008).
7. Ibid.
8. Ibid.
9. Frye, personal correspondence.
10. C. Thompson, *Anatomy of the Soul* (Carol Stream, Ill., Tyndale House Publishers, 2010), 113.
11. T. Clinton and J. Straub, *God Attachment* (New York: Howard Books, 2010), 68.
12. Frye, personal correspondence.
13. Clinton and Straub, *God Attachment,* 69-70
14. Ibid., 70-72.
15. Ibid., 72-73.

16. Ibid., 73-74.
17. U.S. Department of Health and Human Services Assistant Secretary for Planning and Evaluation, "Infant Attachment: What We Know Now," 1991.
18. Frye, personal correspondence.
19. Ibid.
20. Ibid.
21. Merriam-Webster Dictionary Online <http://www.merriam-webster.com/dictionary/nomad>.
22. M. Laaser, *Talking to Your Kids About Sex: How to Have a Lifetime of Age-Appropriate Conversations with Your Children About Healthy Sexuality* (Colorado Springs: WaterBrook Press, 1999), xiv.

Chapter 8
1. Laaser, *Talking to Your Kids About Sex*, 70-85.
2. Ibid., 86-117.
3. Ibid., 118-156.
4. Ibid., 157-202.
5. Daly, personal correspondence.

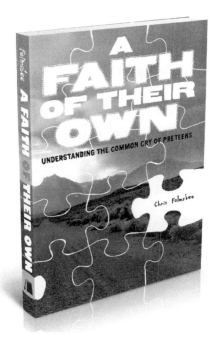